FROM
Warehouse
TO
Your House

■ ■ ■ ■ ■

More Than 250 Simple, Spectacular

Recipes to Cook, Store and Share

When You Buy in Volume

SALLY SAMPSON

SIMON & SCHUSTER PAPERBACKS
New York   London   Toronto   Sydney

SIMON & SCHUSTER
Rockefeller Center
1230 Avenue of the Americas
New York, NY 10020

First Simon & Schuster paperpack edition 2006

SIMON & SCHUSTER and colophon are trademarks
of Simon & Schuster, Inc.

For information about special discounts for bulk purchases,
please contact Simon & Schuster Special Sales at
1-800-456-6798 or business@simonandschuster.com.

Designed by Dana Sloan

Manufactured in the United States of America

10 9 8 7 6 5 4 3 2 1

Library of Congress Cataloging-in-Publication Data

Sampson, Sally.
From warehouse to your house : more than 250 simple, spectacular recipes to
cook, store, and share when you buy in volume / Sally Sampson
p.   cm.
1. Cookery. 2. Frozen foods. 3. Customer clubs. I. Title.

TX714.S255   2006
641.5—dc22   2006050472

ISBN-13: 978-0-7432-7505-7
ISBN-10:   0-7432-7505-5

FROM
Warehouse
TO
Your House

■ ■ ■ ■ ■

More Than 250 Simple, Spectacular
Recipes to Cook, Store and Share
When You Buy in Volume

SALLY SAMPSON

SIMON & SCHUSTER PAPERBACKS
New York   London   Toronto   Sydney

SIMON & SCHUSTER
Rockefeller Center
1230 Avenue of the Americas
New York, NY 10020

First Simon & Schuster paperpack edition 2006

SIMON & SCHUSTER and colophon are trademarks
of Simon & Schuster, Inc.

For information about special discounts for bulk purchases,
please contact Simon & Schuster Special Sales at
1-800-456-6798 or business@simonandschuster.com.

Designed by Dana Sloan

Manufactured in the United States of America

10 9 8 7 6 5 4 3 2 1

Library of Congress Cataloging-in-Publication Data

Sampson, Sally.
From warehouse to your house : more than 250 simple, spectacular recipes to
cook, store, and share when you buy in volume / Sally Sampson
p.   cm.
1. Cookery. 2. Frozen foods. 3. Customer clubs. I. Title.

TX714.S255 2006
641.5—dc22   2006050472

ISBN-13: 978-0-7432-7505-7
ISBN-10:   0-7432-7505-5

For Lauren and Ben, without whom there is no "House"
to bring groceries home to.

Acknowledgments

I thank all my friends and family, who so willingly eat my experiments: Donna Levin and Russ Robinson, David Zebny, Lizzy Shaw, Cynthia Stuart, Steve Steinberg, Saul Nirenberg and Julie Lewit, Sue Nirenberg, Peter and Annette Nirenberg, Susan Orlean and John Gillespie, Judi Fitts, Toby and Sandra Fairbank, Jenny DeBell and Schnig, Toni Bowerman and Dan Oberholzer, Susan Benett and Linette Liebling.

I especially thank my pal Nancy Olin, who not only ate the experiments: she also helped test, shop and critique. Honestly, I couldn't have possibly completed this book without her. And certainly it wouldn't have been nearly as much fun.

I also thank Zach Demuth, for helping with research.

Thanks always and again to my brilliant editor, Sydny Miner, and my equally brilliant agent, Carla Glasser, and her assistant, Jenny Alperen.

Contents

Introduction

The first time I went to a warehouse club, I went with my friend John Schaub, a true devotee and father of four who needs a home filled with stockpiles of food and supplies. I really just wanted to see what the fuss was all about and hadn't intended to buy anything. I was intrigued, but cautious, and purchased a very small amount of food. The second visit I bought a bit more, and by the third time I had my own membership and bought everything I could lay my hands on without thinking about what I really needed. After several days I did what everyone else does: I threw half of it out. The next time I also bought too much food but at least got it into the freezer in time. I hadn't actually cooked any of it but I figured that frozen chicken and ribs were better than no chicken and no ribs.

After a few trips like that, I got smart and learned how to use my purchases quickly and creatively. Six pounds of boneless chicken breasts turned into New-Fangled Classic Chicken Noodle Soup, Curried Chicken Salad for lunch and Moroccan Chicken for the freezer. Six pounds of bone-in chicken breasts became three portions of Jamaican Jerk Chicken (one for the next day, two marinating in the freezer to be cooked after they thawed) and a three-pack of rib-eye steaks got divided and frozen as individual steaks. I turned three pounds of unsalted butter (which of course could just get frozen as is) into Anchovy Butter and Cilantro Butter (for the frozen steaks) and Chocolate Chip Cookies: a batch baked right away, a batch of dough for the fridge and a batch for the freezer. In the meantime, I also opened the gallon jug of extra-virgin olive oil and made Lemon Pepper Dressing and Balsamic Vinaigrette.

I seemed always to buy a ton of stuff: it made me stretch my limits, culinarily speaking. Sometimes I came home and spent the afternoon cleaning and chopping and had all four burners going at once. A huge stack of beef cubes was transformed into Beef Bourguignon, a mountain of ground beef was simmered for Traditional Meat Sauce, a 40-ounce box of button mushrooms turned into Cream of Mushroom Soup, and a package of boned chicken thighs inspired a dish of Braised Chicken Thighs with Escarole for a future dinner party. Pounds of flour and sugar became dough for Citrus Shortbread, Brown Sugar Cookies and Mexican Wedding Cookies. (Once I have my mixer out I might as well take advantage of it.) I filled my own family's bellies, my freezer, and my friends' freezers and took food to those who had broken limbs, broken hearts, achy joints, new babies, or were just overwhelmed by life.

I found that I was becoming more and more creative, was making loads of people happy (never a bad thing) and, not incidentally, had a freezer full of food for myself. When I didn't feel like cooking, I had only to defrost something yummy. It became effortless to invite people over with little notice: I always had enough really good food to share with guests.

The recipes in this book are simple (but interesting), easy to prepare (but range in prep time from literally minutes to days) and pleasurable to cook and eat. While I *almost* always love to cook, when I don't have the time or the inclination, I am so happy to be able to relax and merely open my freezer door.

And speaking of freezers, I have to admit that I started my cooking career being *violently* opposed to freezing anything other than the obvious: ice cream and ice cubes. But as I got busier and busier and had two children, I started to sneak in a few things: butter, bread and sometimes chicken. I discovered that they were fine and gradually, over time, added more and more ingredients to my freezer.

MY RULES

KEEP A HUGE SUPPLY OF RESEALABLE PLASTIC BAGS IN ALL SIZES. Use the bags intended for the freezer when you're freezing: it makes a big difference. Square plastic freezer containers are better than round ones because you can stack them next to each other and not waste space.

LABEL ITEMS IN YOUR FREEZER with a permanent marker (they can be found in the office supply aisle): write down what's in the bag and the date you froze it. Also, if the item requires a garnish or special cooking instructions, put that on the label so you don't have to go back to the recipe.

CHILL HOT FOODS BEFORE YOU FREEZE THEM. Don't put a hot container directly in the freezer. The outer edges will freeze and the center will stay warm for too long.

FREEZE IN PORTIONS. For example, if you live alone, freeze 8 chicken breasts in 8 separate bags. If there are four of you, freeze them in 2 bags, and if you love leftovers, freeze them in one large bag.

FREEZE THINGS FLAT. If you are freezing 4 chicken breasts, lay them out in a single layer and press the air out of the bag before you seal it. For soups and sauces, stand a bag in a bowl and fold the edges down over the outside rim. Fill the bag to within about an inch of the top, then seal the bag and remove it from the bowl. After the bags have frozen flat, stand them up sideways.

AVOID FREEZER BURN by removing as much air as possible: place food in a resealable plastic bag and then squeeze out the air before sealing it up. If what you're freezing is a liquid or is in liquid, leave about an inch of room for expansion.

DON'T STAND IN FRONT OF YOUR FREEZER (or your fridge) and stare at the contents: the less the freezer is opened the more stable the temperature, which guards against freezer burn.

THAW OVERNIGHT IN THE FRIDGE. If you need to rush things, place the entire bag in a bowl of cold water and turn it from time to time. When thawing something that has been marinated, turn or shake the bag occasionally. This will help it marinate evenly.

DON'T THAW IN THE MICROWAVE UNLESS YOU'RE DESPERATE. I am not a fan of using the microwave for defrosting. It's easy for a microwave to thaw unevenly and keep some parts frozen while cooking others.

Essential Ingredients

Warehouse clubs don't sell everything and even if they did, there are some things you don't necessarily want to buy in huge quantities. Whether you're stocking your shelves from a warehouse club, a grocery store or a specialty store, you'll find that if you have a full larder, shopping and cooking become much easier.

IN THE PANTRY

CANNED GOODS:

Beans: black, dark red kidney, and white cannellini

Tomatoes: crushed, diced, and whole peeled Italian plum

Tomato paste

Anchovies

Tuna, water-packed

Chicken broth

DRY GOODS:

All-purpose flour

Sugar: granulated, light brown, and confectioners'

Kosher salt

Baking powder

Baking soda

Sun-dried tomatoes

Pasta: various shapes and sizes

Rice: white, arborio

IN BOTTLES AND JARS:

Oils: olive, extra-virgin olive, canola

Vinegar: red wine, balsamic, white wine, white (distilled)

Worcestershire sauce

Tabasco sauce

Capers

Dijon mustard

Mayonnaise

Toasted sesame oil

Vietnamese chili garlic sauce

Soy sauce

Marinated artichoke hearts

ALCOHOL:

Dry red wine

Dry sherry

Dry white wine

Ale; beer

Dry white vermouth

IN THE FRIDGE:

Eggs, large

Milk

Cream

Parmesan cheese

FRUITS AND VEGETABLES

IN THE FRIDGE:

Carrots

Celery

Ginger

Lemons

Limes

IN THE PANTRY:

Garlic

Potatoes

Red onions

Spanish onions

IN THE FREEZER

Bacon

Unsalted butter

Nuts (all kinds)

Artichoke hearts

DRIED HERBS AND SPICES

As long as they are kept tightly covered and stored in a dark, cool place, spices are considered to have a very long shelf life, but the best way to tell is to smell them. If they don't smell like what they are, toss them.

Basil

Bay leaves

Cayenne pepper

Chili powder

Cinnamon

Cumin

Curry powder

Hungarian paprika

Marjoram

Nutmeg

Oregano

Peppercorns

Red pepper flakes

Rosemary

Sage

Thyme

Essential Equipment

Food processor

Blender

Electric mixer, standing or handheld

Assorted stainless steel mixing bowls

Assorted glass or ceramic bowls

LITTLE STUFF

Ladles

Spoons, wooden and metal

Measuring cups

Measuring spoons

Rubber spatulas

Salad spinner

Stainless steel colander

Pot holders

Whisk

Kitchen shears (great for deboning poultry, trimming fat, snipping herbs, trimming vegetables)

Microplane grater

Can opener

Cheese grater

POTS AND PANS

9-inch cast-iron skillet

8-quart stockpot

2-quart saucepan

5-quart saucepan

Shallow roasting pan

8-inch skillet

10-inch skillet

BAKING

Baking sheet, rimless
Baking sheet, rimmed
8-inch square pan
Bundt pan
9 x 13-inch pan

Basics

This section could as easily be called Building Blocks. These few recipes, including Chicken Stock (below), and Croutons (page 13), are essential to have in your repertoire and are included in many of the recipes in the following chapters.

Chicken Stock

Homemade chicken stock is an essential component of first-rate chicken soup, but you definitely don't need it for every soup, particularly the heartier ones. That said, it's a good idea to keep a handy supply in your freezer. Chicken stock can be cooled and frozen in ice cube trays: as soon as they're solid, transfer them to resealable plastic bags. Or freeze the whole recipe in a resealable plastic bag (see page 2).

The only unpleasant thing about making chicken stock is the inevitable fat layer that forms on the top. The easiest way to degrease a soup is to refrigerate it. When it has completely cooled, the fat will rise to the top and solidify. Simply lift it off and discard it. It's okay if you leave a little behind.

Alternatively, if you want to degrease the stock immediately, take a dry, white, un-decorated paper towel and lay it on top of the stock. Let it absorb the fat for about 5 seconds, then lift it off and discard. Repeat until all the grease appears to be gone, usually about three times.

BAY LEAVES have a strong, distinctive, aromatic, slightly spicy-minty flavor. They don't soften and aren't for eating, so be sure to remove them before serving.

YIELD: ABOUT 20 CUPS

Carcass from 2 chickens, each 6–7 pounds
4 celery stalks, halved
4 carrots, halved
2 parsnips, halved (optional)
2 Spanish onions, quartered
2 bay leaves
2 teaspoons dried thyme
1 teaspoon kosher salt, or more to taste

Place all the ingredients, except the salt, in a large stockpot and cover generously with cold water. Cook, partially covered, over medium heat until the mixture comes to a slow boil. Lower the heat to very low and continue cooking, partially covered, for 3 hours. Do not let it boil again.

Strain the stock and discard the solids. Transfer to a large container, cover and refrigerate until the stock has completely cooled. Lift off and discard the hardened fat. Cover and refrigerate up to 3 days or freeze up to 6 months.

Roasted Garlic

Cooking garlic for a long time mellows its bite. Roasted garlic can be added to mashed potatoes and roasted vegetables, or it can be mashed into a paste to put on bread, steak or chicken.

Do not refrigerate garlic and be sure not to use cloves (sections) that have soft spots or protruding green shoots. When recipes call for garlic, don't substitute powdered or granulated garlic, which pale in flavor.

1 head garlic
1 tablespoon olive oil
¼ teaspoon kosher salt

Preheat the oven to 450 degrees.

Remove as much of the paper from the garlic as possible, being careful to keep the head intact. Rub with the olive oil and sprinkle with the salt. Place on a large piece of aluminum foil and seal the foil so that it forms a packet.

Place in the oven and cook until the garlic is soft and tender, about 45 minutes. When the garlic is cool enough to handle, squeeze the cloves out of the peel into a small bowl, and if using as a puree, mash with a fork. Use immediately, or cover and refrigerate up to 5 days.

Caramelized Onions

Somewhat sweet, somewhat nutty, caramelized onions are a versatile and outstanding addition to pasta, hamburgers, sandwiches, pizzas, omelets and frittatas, and a fine substitute for raw onions in salads.

There are probably as many strategies for avoiding tears when cutting onions as there are cooks. The best defense is to use a really sharp straight-edged knife, but some of the others include good ventilation; peeling them under cold running water; cutting the root off last; refrigerating before cutting; and the silliest of all, chewing gum while peeling. If you're really sensitive and have a lot of onions to cut, wear goggles.

YIELD: ¾–1 CUP

2 tablespoons olive oil

2 large red, Spanish or sweet onions, thinly sliced

2 garlic cloves, minced or thinly sliced (optional)

1 tablespoon minced fresh rosemary leaves

½ teaspoon kosher salt, or more to taste

Place a large skillet over low heat and when it is hot, add the olive oil. Add the remaining ingredients and cook until the onions are deeply browned and slightly gooey, about 40 minutes. If the onions dry out, add water, 1 tablespoon at a time. Stir occasionally but not too much.

Bread Crumbs

> "The smell of good bread baking, like the sound of lightly flowing water, is indescribable in its evocation of innocence and delight."
> —M. F. K. FISHER, WRITER (1908–1992)

YIELD: ABOUT 2 CUPS

Fresh

4 slices stale white or French bread, with or without crusts, cut into quarters

Place the bread in a food processor fitted with a steel blade and pulse until it forms small pieces.

Toasted

1 recipe Fresh Bread Crumbs (see above)

2 tablespoons olive oil or melted unsalted butter

½ teaspoon kosher salt

(Continued on next page)

Preheat the oven to 325 degrees.

Place the fresh bread crumbs in a small bowl, drizzle with the olive oil and gently toss until well coated with the oil. Sprinkle with the salt. Place in a single layer on a baking sheet. Transfer to the oven and bake until golden brown, 10–12 minutes. Set aside to cool. Use immediately, cover and refrigerate up to 1 week, or freeze in a resealable plastic bag up to 2 months.

Toasted Nuts

Toasting nuts greatly improves and intensifies their flavor. While cooking them in a pan is quicker, baking them in the oven results in greater overall consistency and less likelihood of burning them.

SHELLED NUTS can be frozen for 1 year in a resealable plastic bag.

1–4 cups pecans, walnuts, almonds, hazelnuts or pine nuts

Preheat the oven to 300 degrees.

Place the nuts in a single layer on a rimmed baking sheet. Transfer to the oven and bake until golden brown, 10–12 minutes.

Alternatively, place the nuts in a large skillet over medium heat and cook, stirring frequently, until golden brown and aromatic, about 5 minutes.

Set aside to cool. Use immediately, or transfer to a resealable plastic bag and refrigerate up to 1 month or freeze up to 1 year.

Croutons

Any kind of bread can be used for croutons, but the ones I suggest below are the most typical. For something more unusual I especially like leftover corn bread, pumpernickel, and rustic breads with dried fruit and nuts or olives.

YIELD: ABOUT 4–5 CUPS

4–5 cups ½-inch cubes of French, Italian or white bread
2 tablespoons olive oil
2 garlic cloves, minced
1 teaspoon kosher salt
1 tablespoon finely grated Parmesan or Romano cheese (optional)

Preheat the oven to 350 degrees.

Place the bread, olive oil, garlic, salt and cheese, if desired, in a bowl and toss to combine. Place in a single layer on a baking sheet. Transfer to the oven and bake until golden brown, 15–20 minutes. Set aside to cool. Use immediately, cover and refrigerate up to 1 week, or freeze in a resealable plastic bag up to 6 months.

Roasted Peppers

Roasted peppers are great on an antipasto platter, used in salads in place of raw peppers, spooned atop burgers or stuffed into sandwiches and omelets.

6 bell peppers, any color

Preheat the broiler.

Cut off the top and the bottom of each pepper; then slit the pepper open and discard the stem, ribs and seeds. Flatten each pepper out so that it resembles a small piece of paper.

Place the peppers, shiny side up, directly under the broiler, as close together as possible and cook until blackened, 5 to 7 minutes. While still hot, remove the peppers and place in a heavy plastic or paper bag, close shut and let sweat for about 10 minutes. Remove and discard the burned skin. Set aside to cool. Cover and refrigerate up to 3 weeks.

Starters

"If you cannot do great things, do small things in a great way."

—NAPOLEON HILL, WRITER (1883–1970)

I am not a fan of little bits of food. I am not interested in spending tons of time doing things like stuffing mushrooms (although I do make an exception for the date recipe that follows) but instead like to make interesting but relatively simple things to start a meal.

Spiced Walnuts/Pecans

Perfect for gift giving, especially around the holidays, these nuts have a shelf life of six months. While it's a rare household that doesn't consume these the day they're made, it's nice to know this recipe doesn't have to be made the night before an event.

You can substitute an equal amount of curry powder, or 3 teaspoons black pepper, plus ¼ teaspoon cayenne pepper, for the cinnamon or pumpkin pie spice.

PUMPKIN PIE SPICE is typically a combination of ground cinnamon, ginger, nutmeg, all-spice, mace and cloves. The proportions vary depending on the spice company. It can also be used as a substitute for or an addition to cinnamon in foods like banana bread and carrot cake. This mixture is a great shortcut for cooks at Thanksgiving.

> "I'm nuts and I know it. But so long as I make 'em laugh, they ain't going to lock me up."
>
> —RED SKELTON, AMERICAN COMEDIAN (1913–1997)

YIELD: ABOUT 4 CUPS

4 cups walnuts or pecans, or a combination
1 large egg white
1 teaspoon cold water
¾ cup sugar
1 teaspoon kosher salt
2 teaspoons ground cinnamon or pumpkin pie spice

Preheat the oven to 225 degrees. Line a rimmed baking sheet with parchment paper.

Place the nuts, egg white and water in a bowl and toss until the nuts are well coated. Add the sugar, salt and cinnamon and toss again.

Place on the prepared sheet and transfer to the oven. Bake, stirring every 15 minutes, until the nuts appear dry, about 1 hour. Set aside to cool and serve immediately, or store in a resealable plastic bag in the freezer for up to 6 months.

Bruschetta

I often seem to have the luck to arrive at the store just when the bread has come out of the oven, and inevitably I am seduced by the smell and buy too much. As a result, I am often left with more bread than we can consume in a day or two. Instead of bemoaning the fact that it's no longer oven-fresh, I take advantage of my bounty by slicing it up and popping it in the freezer. This way, when I need a quick appetizer, I'm ready.

BRUSCHETTA is one of the many brilliant solutions Italians have devised for day-old bread. It is simply toasted bread, usually brushed with oil and garlic. You can use any kind of crusty rustic bread, but I wouldn't use a packaged sandwich bread.

SERVES 4–6

2 garlic cloves, finely minced
2 tablespoons olive oil
16–20 thick slices French or Italian bread (about 1 loaf)
Kosher salt

Prepare a grill or preheat the oven.

Place the garlic and olive oil in a small bowl and set aside.

Toast or grill the bread slices until golden brown. Remove the slices, brush with the olive oil and sprinkle with salt.

Tomato and Arugula Bruschetta

6 plum or 4 beefsteak tomatoes, seeded and diced or sliced
¼ cup Balsamic Vinaigrette (page 67)
16 arugula leaves (optional)
Kosher salt

If you have the time, after you slice the tomatoes, place them in a small nonreactive bowl with the balsamic vinaigrette for at least 1 hour and up to 4 hours. Before proceeding, drain them well and discard the vinaigrette.

Prepare a grill or preheat the oven.

Toast or grill the bread slices until golden brown. Remove the slices, brush with the oil, top with the tomatoes, vinaigrette and arugula, if desired, and sprinkle with salt.

Roasted Pepper and Anchovy Bruschetta

2 roasted red bell peppers (page 13), chopped
6 anchovy fillets, chopped
¼ cup chopped fresh Italian flat-leaf parsley leaves
Coarsely ground black pepper

Prepare a grill or preheat the oven.

Place the red peppers, anchovy fillets and parsley in a bowl and mix to combine.

Toast or grill the bread slices until golden brown. Remove the slices, brush with the oil, top each with 1 tablespoon of the roasted pepper mixture and sprinkle with black pepper.

Fresh Mozzarella and Tomato Bruschetta

2 medium balls fresh mozzarella, thinly sliced
6 plum or 4 beefsteak tomatoes, seeded and diced or sliced
Kosher salt
Coarsely ground black pepper

Prepare a grill or preheat the oven.

Toast or grill the bread slices until golden brown. Remove the slices, brush with the oil and top with the mozzarella. Add the tomatoes and then sprinkle with salt and pepper.

Prosciutto, Mozzarella and Arugula Bruschetta

2 medium balls fresh mozzarella, thinly sliced
8–12 slices prosciutto, halved
16 arugula leaves
Balsamic vinegar
Kosher salt
Coarsely ground black pepper

Prepare a grill or preheat the oven.

Toast or grill the bread slices until golden brown. Remove the slices, brush with the oil and top with the mozzarella. Add the prosciutto and arugula to each slice, and then drizzle with balsamic vinegar. Sprinkle with salt and pepper.

Garlic Bread

The garlic butter can also be used as a pasta sauce or a garnish for soups, or you can drizzle it over steamed or roasted vegetables or grilled chicken or beef.

> "Without garlic I simply would not care to live."
>
> —LOUIS DIAT, FRENCH CHEF (1885–1958)

SERVES 4–6

For the garlic butter:

¼ cup olive oil

8–10 garlic cloves, minced or chopped

½ cup unsalted butter, at room temperature

½ teaspoon dried oregano

1 teaspoon kosher salt

1 tablespoon chopped fresh basil leaves (optional)

1 tablespoon chopped fresh cilantro leaves (optional)

1 French or Italian baguette, cut into slices

Freshly grated Parmesan cheese (optional)

TO MAKE THE GARLIC BUTTER: Place a large skillet over very low heat and add the olive oil. Add the garlic and cook until tender and lightly colored, 8–10 minutes. Do not let it brown. Set aside to cool for 10 minutes (it will still be slightly warm). Add the butter and combine well. Add the oregano, salt, basil and cilantro, if desired. Mix well and transfer to a small serving bowl, cover, and refrigerate up to 1 month or freeze in a resealable plastic bag up to 3 months.

Toast the bread. Spread with garlic butter and sprinkle with Parmesan cheese, if desired. Serve immediately.

Marinated Mozzarella

Don't substitute the factory-produced supermarket variety for fresh mozzarella. It just won't be the same.

Adding fresh basil leaves and sundried tomatoes, either whole or sliced, will make this more elaborate but very special. Save the oil for drizzling on steamed or roasted vegetables or grilled steak.

FRESH MOZZARELLA (sometimes called *fiore di latte*) is a completely different cheese than American mozzarella. American mozzarella (also called slicing mozzarella) is a semisoft cheese made exclusively from cow's milk and is most often used in cooking for its texture, generally as a topping (in the case of pizza), as a sandwich addition or as a component of a dish; rarely is it eaten alone. Fresh mozzarella, however, is commonly eaten alone or marinated in olive and garlic as an antipasto. Originally made only from water buffalo's milk, in America fresh mozzarella is now made with cow's milk; it is a soft white cheese with a slightly sweet milky flavor. It can be purchased in a block, which can easily be sliced, or in little balls (bocconcini), which can be marinated or eaten plain.

SERVES 6–8

1 pound fresh mozzarella, cut into ½- to ¾-inch cubes, or 1 pound bocconcini
¼ cup extra-virgin or virgin olive oil
¼ teaspoon crushed red pepper flakes
¼ teaspoon kosher salt
1 tablespoon finely chopped fresh basil or Italian flat-leaf parsley leaves,
    or ¼ teaspoon dried basil

Place everything in a bowl and toss well. Cover and refrigerate overnight and up to 2 weeks.

Stuffed Dates

Faced with a brand-new box of dates and half a package of prosciutto (purchased for another dish), my pal Nancy got to work wrapping the prosciutto around the dates. After eating two, she and I decided they'd be even better stuffed with blue cheese, and after two more, we decided they'd be even *better* with the addition of pecans. You'd think we would have had it by then, but we kept eating. And then later, we dreamed of eating them. These are truly amazing, at every stage.

This recipe is written for one date because it's easier to make them one by one, but I would never suggest it's possible to eat just one. Make as many as you think you'll need.

If you like, substitute feta or goat cheese for the blue cheese, and lightly toasted almonds or walnuts for the pecans.

Originally from Morocco, DATES, the oldest fruit cultivated by man, were considered sacred in ancient times. Although their texture and sweetness make them seem rich, dates contain more potassium than bananas, are low in fat and contain no cholesterol. They are also low in sodium and high in fiber and magnesium.

PROSCIUTTO DI PARMA, a specialty of Parma, Italy, is an Italian-style raw ham, cured by dry salting for one month, followed by air-drying in cool curing sheds for about one year. Cut into tissue-thin slices that highlight its intense flavor and deep pink color, Prosciutto di Parma is regarded as the best quality. Prosciutto can be refrigerated, well wrapped, for several weeks.

1 date
½ teaspoon blue cheese
1 pecan, lightly toasted or spiced (pages 12, 16)
½ slice prosciutto

Cut open the date and remove the stone, if not already pitted. Fill the cavity with blue cheese and a pecan and then reform into its original shape. Wrap with prosciutto. Serve immediately, or cover and refrigerate up to overnight. Allow to come to room temperature before serving.

Mango Salsa/Chutney

When I buy a case of mangoes, which I frequently do, it seems we either eat them all within two days or eat two and then forget about them. This recipe is a perfect solution. Fresh, the salsa is perfect for chips of any kind or as a topping for burgers or grilled fish. Cook it over medium heat until it comes together, 30–45 minutes, and you have a chutney. Serve the chutney as an accompaniment to grilled steak or Boston Trio chicken (page 129). As long as they are perfectly ripe (have an aroma and give a bit when you push on them), I find the easiest way to peel a mango is with a potato peeler.

Used most frequently in Indian, Middle Eastern and Scandinavian cooking, CARDAMOM has a flavor that is very difficult to describe, but once you know it you'll never forget it: pungent and sweet with a slight lemony, ginger flavor.

Peel FRESH GINGERROOT using a potato peeler.

MAKES 4–5 CUPS

7–8 perfectly ripe mangoes, peeled, pitted and chopped
1 red bell pepper, diced
½ red onion, chopped
2 tart apples, peeled and diced
½ cup sugar
½ cup white (distilled) vinegar
1 teaspoon ground cardamom
1 tablespoon finely chopped fresh gingerroot
1 teaspoon black pepper
¼ teaspoon cayenne pepper
¼ cup chopped fresh cilantro leaves (optional)

Place everything in a large bowl and mix to combine. Cover and refrigerate at least 4 hours and up to 3 days.

Spicy Red/Black Bean Dip

Spicy, sweet, tart and creamy, this wonderful dip has something for everyone!

YIELD: 1½–2 CUPS

One 15.5-ounce can red kidney or black turtle beans, well rinsed and drained
2 garlic cloves
¼ teaspoon ground cumin
1 chipotle chile in adobo (page 184)
½ teaspoon kosher salt
¼ cup fresh orange juice
Juice of ½ lime
2 tablespoons chopped fresh cilantro leaves

Place the beans, garlic, cumin, chile, salt, orange juice, lime juice and 1 tablespoon cilantro in a food processor fitted with a steel blade and process until smooth.

Transfer to a serving bowl and serve immediately, garnished with the remaining 1 tablespoon cilantro, or cover and refrigerate up to 3 days.

Onion Dip

Move over, Lipton Soup mix. This is a fresh, updated version of the classic dip I grew up on.

New research indicates that strong-tasting onions (yellow and red onions, and shallots too) are packed with cancer-fighting flavonoids.

> "I used to hang out by the food table at parties because you don't have to talk to anybody. If you do then you can talk about the food."
>
> —JENNIFER JASON LEIGH, ACTRESS (B. 1962)

YIELD: 2–2½ CUPS

2 tablespoons unsalted butter
2 red onions, halved and chopped
2 teaspoons chopped fresh rosemary leaves
1 cup sour cream
1 cup mayonnaise
½ teaspoon kosher salt
½ teaspoon black pepper
2 scallion greens, chopped, for garnish

Place a small skillet over low heat and when it is hot, add the butter. Add the onions and rosemary and cook, stirring occasionally, until the onions are deeply browned and caramelized, 35–40 minutes. Transfer to a small mixing bowl and set aside to cool.

Add the sour cream, mayonnaise, salt and pepper, and mix to combine.

Serve immediately, garnished with the scallion greens, or cover and refrigerate up to 2 days.

Goat Cheese and Sundried Tomato Dip

The combination of the mild goat cheese and the intense, sweet flavor of the sundried tomatoes makes an especially tasty dip (plus, it's incredibly quick and almost effortless to assemble). If you buy sundried tomatoes that are not packed in oil, simply soak them overnight in olive oil to plump them.

Serve with pita bread triangles or crudités, as a spread for turkey or roast beef sandwiches, as a topping for burgers, or stuffed into an omelet.

SUNDRIED TOMATOES were originally dried in the sun; they are now dried in low heat ovens. In the '80s it seemed you couldn't order a dish without having them included and I came to loathe them. Now I enjoy them and particularly love them here.

> "I don't want the cheese, I just want to get out of the trap."
> —SPANISH PROVERB

YIELD: ABOUT 2 CUPS

1 log plain soft goat cheese (about 8 inches long), at room temperature
⅔–¾ cup sundried tomatoes in oil, finely chopped, oil reserved
½ teaspoon kosher salt
Finely chopped fresh basil leaves, for garnish (optional)

Place the goat cheese and tomatoes in a bowl and mash with a fork. Add 1 tablespoon of the reserved oil and the salt, and mash again. Serve immediately, or cover and refrigerate up to 1 week. Garnish with basil leaves, if desired, just before serving.

Pesto Goat Cheese

Whether you use homemade or store-bought pesto, this is an easy way to transform a log of goat cheese into an interesting spread that can be used for crudités, pita bread triangles, sandwiches, burgers and omelets.

PESTO is a classic Italian sauce made from fresh basil leaves, Parmesan cheese, pine nuts, olive oil, garlic and salt.

YIELD: ABOUT 2 CUPS

1 log plain soft goat cheese (about 8 inches long), at room temperature
½ cup pesto
Finely chopped fresh basil leaves, for garnish (optional)

Place the goat cheese and pesto in a bowl and mash with a fork. Serve immediately, or cover and refrigerate up to 1 week. Garnish with basil leaves just before serving.

Guacamole

The most important element in great guacamole is the avocadoes, which must be perfectly ripe: they should be supple and yield just slightly when you touch them. Since it's rare to find them in this condition, be sure to buy avocadoes at least three to five days ahead of when you want to use them. To accelerate the ripening process, place the avocado in a paper bag with an apple. If it's already ripe enough, either use it (chopped in salads, sliced on a sandwich or burger, or drizzled with balsamic vinaigrette), or simply refrigerate it—it won't continue to ripen in the fridge.

Guacamole can be made a few hours ahead: place a pit in the guacamole and then cover tightly with plastic wrap, making sure the plastic comes in contact with the guacamole. This will prevent the guacamole from turning brown.

Like avocadoes, guacamole is also great in sandwiches, in omelets and on burgers.

It is best to use rubber gloves when chopping JALAPEÑOS. **If you like your guacamole spicy, retain and use the seeds and ribs, and if you don't, discard them.**

YIELD: ABOUT 4½–5 CUPS

6 perfectly ripe avocadoes, coarsely chopped
1 large beefsteak tomato, coarsely chopped
½ bunch scallions, chopped
½ cup chopped fresh cilantro leaves, plus additional for garnish
1 teaspoon cayenne pepper
1 teaspoon kosher salt
¼ teaspoon crushed red pepper flakes
3–4 tablespoons fresh lime juice
½–1 jalapeño pepper or chipotle chile, finely minced (optional)
2 very thin lime slices, for garnish

Place all the ingredients except the lime in a bowl and toss gently to mix. Do not overmix: the guacamole should be somewhat chunky.

Transfer to a serving bowl and serve immediately, or sprinkle with lemon or lime juice and cover with plastic wrap placed directly on top of the guacamole (to prevent discoloration). Refrigerate for up to 8 hours. Serve garnished with the cilantro sprigs and lime slices.

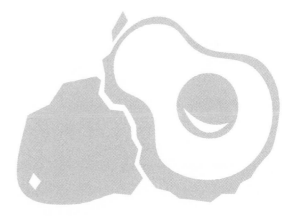

Smoked Salmon Tartare

This unusual but extravagant recipe calls for finely chopped smoked salmon instead of fresh. It's best served atop crackers or small pumpernickel squares spread with unsalted butter, or stuffed inside endive spears.

SERVES 8–10

Classic Version

 1 pound smoked salmon, finely chopped

 ½ red onion, finely chopped

 2 scallions, finely chopped

 3 tablespoons capers, drained

 2 tablespoons finely chopped fresh Italian flat-leaf parsley leaves,
     plus additional for garnish

 1 teaspoon fresh lemon juice or red wine vinegar

 ¼–½ teaspoon black pepper

Place all the ingredients in a small bowl and mix gently. Cover and refrigerate at least 1 hour and up to 6 hours.

Asian-Inspired Version

1 pound smoked salmon, finely chopped

½ red onion, finely chopped

2 scallions, finely chopped

1 teaspoon finely chopped or grated fresh gingerroot

½–1 teaspoon Vietnamese chili garlic sauce

2 tablespoons chopped fresh cilantro leaves

⅛ teaspoon toasted sesame oil

1 teaspoon fresh lime juice or rice vinegar

Place all the ingredients in a small bowl and mix gently. Cover and refrigerate at least 1 hour and up to 6 hours.

VIETNAMESE CHILI GARLIC SAUCE is indispensable in my kitchen. Its primary ingredients are jalapeño chiles, garlic, salt and vinegar. (Look for the green caps and Rooster logo by Huy Fong Foods, www.huyfong.com.) Huy Fong makes two kinds: Tuong Ot Toi Viet-Nam, in a clear squat bottle, and the smoother, hotter Sriracha Chili Sauce, in a squirt bottle. Both are good to keep on hand. When used sparingly, they add a mysterious flavor; when used liberally, they impart terrific heat. Both are available in most city supermarkets and specialty shops. Huy Fong Foods manufactures their sauces in California, not in Asia, as is often assumed.

Betsy's Shrimp

Nancy's aunt Betsy has been making this recipe for many years. Their tradition is that the whole family eats it with cocktails on Thanksgiving and always with Bremner wafers. At my house, we eat it for dinner.

DRY MUSTARD (finely ground mustard seed) was originally used by the Romans and Greeks in the 1st century AD as both a culinary and a medicinal spice. It is much stronger and hotter than prepared mustard, which is mellowed by aging and contains other ingredients, most notably vinegar. Mustard is in the same family as broccoli, Brussels sprouts, kale, kohlrabi and collard greens.

SERVES 6–8

For the marinade:

1 cup canola or mild olive oil, or a combination
1 cup white wine vinegar
¼ cup sugar
¼ cup water
1 teaspoon kosher salt
½ teaspoon whole peppercorns
¼ teaspoon dry mustard
3 bay leaves
2 tablespoons Worcestershire sauce
¼ teaspoon garlic salt (optional)

2 pounds cooked medium-size shrimp
2 sweet onions, such as Vidalia or Walla Walla, thinly sliced
1 lemon, thinly sliced

Place the marinade ingredients in a large bowl or resealable plastic bag and mix well. Add the shrimp, onions and lemon slices. Cover or seal, and refrigerate at least 24 hours and up to 3 days. Stir every once in a while.

Place in a colander, discard the marinade, peppercorns and bay leaves, and serve garnished with onion and lemon slices.

Avocado and Shrimp Salad

This salad is just the thing to serve for a summer lunch or as a starter to a meal. The recipe calls for unadorned shrimp but you can also use Chili-Rubbed Shrimp (page 244) if you have some left over. I like to scoop it up with tortilla chips.

An average LIME supplies 1 to 2 teaspoons grated zest and 2 tablespoons juice. Be careful not to grate any of the white pith: it's very bitter.

SERVES 4

1 pound cooked shrimp, cut into large chunks
Grated zest and juice of 2 limes
3 tablespoons chopped fresh cilantro leaves
2 perfectly ripe avocadoes, cubed
½ cup chopped fresh pineapple or peach
1 large ripe tomato, diced
¼ teaspoon crushed red pepper flakes
½ teaspoon kosher salt

Place all the ingredients in a large glass or ceramic bowl and toss to combine. Cover and refrigerate at least 20 minutes but no longer than 1 hour.

Mozzarella and Tomato Tart

This very simple and delicious tart is perfect for a starter, or as a light lunch or dinner.

This tart freezes well. Unless you own a zillion tart pans, freeze it in the pan, and when it's solid, remove it from the pan and place it in a resealable plastic bag. When you're ready to cook or reheat it, put it back in the tart pan and reheat it for 20 minutes in a 325-degree oven.

There are five main varieties of TOMATOES: cherry, pear, plum, beefsteak and "slicing" tomatoes. "Slicing" tomatoes, the most common variety, consist of all of the large, round tomatoes, which are generally red but can also be yellow. Meaty and juicy with a slightly sweet flavor, they can be eaten alone or sliced in a salad. Beefsteak tomatoes have a similar appearance to "slicing" tomatoes except they are flatter, meatier and less juicy, making them perfect for cooking. Plum tomatoes, also known as Roma tomatoes, are smaller, far less juicy and perfect for making tomato sauce. Both cherry and pear tomatoes are much smaller and have a very sweet flavor. They are generally eaten alone or mixed into a salad.

> "There's no such thing as a free lunch."
> —MILTON FRIEDMAN, ECONOMIST (B.1912)

SERVES 6

For the pastry:

¾ cup plus 2 tablespoons all-purpose flour

¼ teaspoon kosher salt

½ teaspoon sugar

6 tablespoons unsalted butter, chilled and sliced

1 tablespoon plus 1 teaspoon ice water

(Continued on next page)

For the filling:

1 tablespoon Dijon mustard

½ cup ricotta cheese

¼ pound mozzarella cheese, thinly sliced or grated (fresh is better but American-style is fine)

3–4 large ripe tomatoes, thinly sliced

1 garlic clove, minced

1 teaspoon dried oregano

⅛ teaspoon black pepper

2 tablespoons chopped fresh basil leaves

TO MAKE THE PASTRY: Place the flour, salt and sugar in a food processor fitted with a steel blade and pulse to blend. Add the butter, one slice at a time, and mix until crumbly and no clumps of butter remain. Add the water and mix until a ball forms, about 30 seconds. Form the dough into a disk, wrap it in plastic wrap or waxed paper, and refrigerate until firm, at least 1 hour.

Preheat the oven to 325 degrees.

Sprinkle flour on the countertop, place the dough on it, and using a rolling pin, roll it out into a 10-inch circle. Place it in a 9-inch tart pan. If you are using a 9-inch pie pan, crimp the edges about halfway up the sides: this is a shallow tart. Cover the dough with aluminum foil or waxed paper and fill with pie weights or beans. Bake for 10 minutes. Remove the foil and weights and bake for 10–12 additional minutes.

Raise the temperature to 400 degrees. Line the crust with the mustard and then with the ricotta. Sprinkle with the mozzarella and place the tomato slices in a circular pattern. Sprinkle with the garlic, oregano and pepper. Place in the oven and bake for 45 minutes. Sprinkle with the basil as soon as it comes out of the oven. Serve immediately or at room temperature.

Caramelized Onion Tart

This versatile tart can be served in large slices as a lunch or supper dish, accompanied by a green salad. In small slices, it makes a nice starter for a dinner party, and in even smaller slices, a tasty snack to serve with cocktails.

The tart can be frozen: follow the instructions for freezing and reheating the Mozzarella and Tomato Tart (page 35).

> "Life is like an onion. You peel it off one layer at a time; and sometimes you weep."　　—CARL SANDBURG, POET (1878–1967)

SERVES 6

For the pastry:

¾ cup plus 2 tablespoons all-purpose flour

¼ teaspoon kosher salt

½ teaspoon sugar

6 tablespoons unsalted butter, chilled and sliced

1 tablespoon plus 1 teaspoon ice water

For the filling:

1 cup grated mozzarella cheese

1 cup goat cheese

1 recipe Caramelized Onions (page 10)

½ teaspoon dried thyme or rosemary

⅛ teaspoon black pepper

TO MAKE THE PASTRY: Place the flour, salt and sugar in a food processor fitted with a steel blade and pulse to blend. Add the butter, one slice at a time, and mix until crum-

(Continued on next page)

bly and no clumps of butter remain. Add the water and mix until a ball forms, about 30 seconds. Form the dough into a disk, wrap it in plastic wrap or waxed paper, and refrigerate until firm, at least 1 hour.

Preheat the oven to 325 degrees.

Sprinkle flour on the countertop, place the dough on it, and using a rolling pin, roll it out into a 10-inch circle. Place it in a 9-inch tart pan. If you are using a 9-inch pie pan, crimp the edges about halfway up the sides: this is a shallow tart. Cover the dough with aluminum foil or waxed paper and fill with pie weights or beans. Bake for 10 minutes. Remove the foil and weights and bake for 10–12 additional minutes.

Raise the temperature to 400 degrees. Line the crust with the mozzarella cheese. Sprinkle with the goat cheese and top with the caramelized onions. Sprinkle with the thyme and pepper. Place in the oven and bake for 15 minutes. Serve immediately or at room temperature.

Soups and Chilis

"There is nothing like soup. It is by nature eccentric: no two are ever alike, unless of course you get your soup in a can."

—LAURIE COLWIN, WRITER (1944–1992)

Most people who love soup have recipes and memories from their childhood. Although my mother was a great cook and we always ate together as a family, I have no recollection of her ever actually making soup from scratch. I do remember eating soup often when I was sick—Campbell's Cream of Tomato and Campbell's Cream of Celery are clear in my mind—so I suppose soups still meant comfort to me. Today soups and chilis are my favorite foods to make, and fortunately I live in a home of adventurous eaters who are happy to consume them. Although it takes a long time to cook, soup takes little time to prepare. It can sit in the fridge for a day or two and gets better as it stands. It is easily frozen and easily defrosted. I usually freeze soup in plastic containers but when I make a lot or want to save space. I freeze it flat in resealable plastic bags.

Share soup with your friends: it will make them really happy!

True Classic Chicken Noodle Soup

This is one recipe you *must* have in your collection. My daughter, Lauren, says, "It's great in the winter. It warms your bones and makes you feel all happy." The possibilities are infinite: vary the fresh herbs, or add chopped tomatoes or crushed red pepper flakes.

YIELD: ABOUT 12 CUPS

1 tablespoon unsalted butter or olive oil

One 5-pound roaster chicken, cut up into parts

1 onion, halved and finely chopped

1 celery stalk, sliced

2–3 carrots, sliced or diced

1 parsnip, sliced or diced (optional)

1 teaspoon finely chopped fresh gingerroot

1 garlic clove, pressed or finely chopped

10 cups Chicken Stock (page 8)

¼ cup small pasta (such as alphabet or orzo), rice or barley, *or* 1 large potato, diced

1–2 tablespoons chopped fresh dill leaves

Kosher salt

Black pepper

Place a large heavy-bottomed soup pot over medium heat and when it is hot, add the butter. When the butter has melted, add the chicken and cook until well browned on all sides, about 10 minutes total. Set the chicken aside. Add the onion, vegetables, ginger and garlic to the pot and cook, covered, until the vegetables are tender, 10–15 minutes.

Add the chicken stock and reserved chicken pieces, raise the heat to high and bring to a gentle boil. Lower the heat to low and cook, partially covered, until the chicken is falling off the bone, 1–1½ hours. Remove the chicken to a plate.

When cool enough to handle, remove and discard the chicken skin and bones and return the chicken meat to the pot. Transfer the soup to a container, cover and refrigerate at least 4 hours and up to 3 days. When the fat solidifies at the top of the soup, remove and discard it. The soup can be frozen at this point. (To serve the soup without chilling it first, degrease it as described on page 8.)

To reheat the soup, place it in a pot, add the pasta and bring to a low boil over low heat. Cook until the pasta is tender, about 10 minutes (add 15 minutes to cooking time if using rice or barley). Add the dill and salt and pepper to taste. Serve immediately.

New-Fangled Classic Chicken Noodle Soup

While the true classic is made with a whole chicken, here is a version that requires less time and effort but is still fabulous. Instead of cooking the poultry in the soup, you can use leftover poached chicken or turkey.

> "Only the pure in heart can make a good soup."
> —LUDWIG VAN BEETHOVEN, COMPOSER (1770–1827)

YIELD: 10–12 CUPS

1 tablespoon unsalted butter or olive oil

1 Spanish onion, halved and finely chopped

2 celery stalks, sliced or diced

2 carrots, sliced or diced

1 teaspoon dried marjoram, or 1 tablespoon chopped fresh marjoram leaves

1 teaspoon dried rosemary, or 1 tablespoon chopped fresh rosemary leaves

¼ teaspoon dried thyme, or 1 teaspoon chopped fresh thyme leaves

10 cups Chicken Stock (page 8)

½ cup rice or small pasta (such as alphabet or orzo)

1 pound boneless, skinless chicken breast halves, diced

Place a large heavy-bottomed soup pot over medium heat and when it is hot, add the butter. When the butter has melted, add the onion, celery, carrots and dried herbs (if using) and cook until tender, 10–15 minutes.

Add the chicken stock, raise the heat to high and bring to a boil. Lower the heat to low and cook, uncovered, 1 hour. The soup can be cooled and frozen at this point.

Add the rice and cook until tender, about 20 minutes.

Add the chicken, stir, and cook until cooked completely, 8–10 minutes. If you are using fresh herbs, add them now. Serve immediately, or cover and refrigerate up to 3 days.

Avgolemono

This lemony soup is the Greek equivalent to Grandma's chicken soup: soothing, homey and just what the doctor orders when you're sick.

LONG-GRAIN RICE includes jasmine and basmati varieties. The kernels are slender: four or five times as long as they are wide. It is less glutinous than short-grain Asian and Italian rice, and separates easily.

> "It is probable that the lemon is the most valuable of all fruit for pre-serving health."
>
> —MAUD GRIEVE, HERBALIST AND AUTHOR

YIELD: 8–10 CUPS

12 cups Chicken Stock (page 8)
½ cup long-grain white rice or orzo
12 large egg yolks
⅓–½ cup fresh lemon juice
⅓ cup chopped fresh Italian flat-leaf parsley, mint or dill leaves, or a combination

Place the chicken stock in a medium-size soup pot and bring to a boil over high heat. Add the rice, lower the heat to low and cook until the rice is tender, about 15 minutes.

Place the egg yolks and lemon juice in a bowl and whisk together; the mixture tends to come out a little better if done by hand, rather than in a food processor or blender.

Very gradually, add some of the stock to the lemon mixture, being very careful not to let the eggs curdle. Return the mixture to the soup pot and cook over very low heat for 10 minutes. Keep whisking until all the stock is combined with the eggs.

Serve immediately, garnished with the herbs, or cover and refrigerate up to 3 days. Reheat gently over low heat.

Carrot Soup with Orange

A perfect starter for dinner, Carrot Soup with Orange is rich in flavor yet light and refreshing.

Apple cider or apple juice can be substituted for the orange juice.

> "An idealist is one who, on noticing that a rose smells better than a cabbage, concludes that it will also make better soup."
>
> —H. L. MENCKEN, JOURNALIST AND WRITER (1880–1956)

YIELD: ABOUT 12 CUPS

1 tablespoon olive or canola oil
1 Spanish onion, halved and chopped
2 garlic cloves, minced
2–3 teaspoons finely chopped fresh gingerroot
2 pounds carrots, cut in chunks
8 cups Chicken Stock (page 8) or vegetable broth
1 cup orange juice

Place a large heavy-bottomed soup pot over medium-high heat and when it is hot, add the olive oil. Add the onion, garlic and ginger and cook until the onion is soft, 5–7 minutes. Raise the heat to high, add the carrots and chicken stock and bring to a boil. Lower the heat to low and cook until the carrots are soft, about 20 minutes.

Transfer the soup, in batches, to a blender or a food processor fitted with a steel blade, and puree until completely smooth. Just prior to serving, add the orange juice and cook until heated through.

Serve immediately, or cover and refrigerate up to 5 days or freeze up to 2 months. (If freezing, it is best to omit the orange juice, and add it when reheating.)

Red Pepper Soup

When I see those colorful bags of peppers in the store, I buy them assuming I am going to eat them all raw, in salads and with dips. Of course, this is often not possible, and this unusual soup is a great way to use them if you are a bell pepper fan like me! This soup is best served on the day it is made.

You can spice it up with crushed red pepper flakes or almost any kind of hot sauce. Additionally, if you halve the amount of chicken stock, it makes a great sauce for almost any medium-size shaped pasta.

YIELD: 8–10 CUPS

1 tablespoon unsalted butter
1 Spanish onion, halved and coarsely chopped
2 red bell peppers, cut into wide strips
2 green bell peppers, cut into wide strips
2 yellow bell peppers, cut into wide strips
One 16-ounce can diced tomatoes, including the liquid
8–10 cups Chicken Stock (page 8)
1–2 teaspoons Dijon mustard
1 cup heavy or light cream, sour cream or plain yogurt
¼ cup chopped fresh dill, cilantro or basil leaves, plus additional for garnish
Black pepper

Place a large heavy-bottomed soup pot over medium heat and when it is hot, add the butter. When the butter has melted, add the onion and peppers and cook until tender, 10–15 minutes.

Using a slotted spoon, transfer the onion and peppers to a food processor fitted with a steel blade. Pulse until they are bite-size. Return them to the soup pot. Add the tomatoes, stock and mustard, raise the heat to high and bring to a boil. Lower the heat to low and simmer for 10 minutes.

Gradually add the cream, dill and pepper to taste, stirring all the while. Serve immediately, garnished with the additional herbs.

Gazpacho

This refreshing raw summer soup is a salad in a bowl. The classic Spanish recipe has more olive oil and includes bread crumbs; this version uses less oil and substitutes croutons for the crumbs, reducing the calories and improving the flavor and texture. Dill and cilantro aren't traditional Spanish flavors, but both work in this recipe. The feta isn't traditional either, but it adds a great contrast.

My son, Ben, says he isn't a soup lover but he loves gazpacho because it's cold and spicy.

This soup cannot be frozen.

SHERRY VINEGAR, at once tart, sweet and nutty, gives this soup an extra layer of flavor. However, if you don't have any, red wine vinegar is a perfectly acceptable substitute.

YIELD: 10–12 CUPS

2 English cucumbers, cut into ¼-inch dice

2 large perfectly ripe vine-ripened tomatoes, cut into ¼-inch dice

1 small red, Vidalia or Spanish onion, halved and coarsely chopped

2–4 garlic cloves, minced

2 red, orange or yellow bell peppers, cut into ¼-inch dice

2 tablespoons olive oil

3–4 tablespoons sherry vinegar or red wine vinegar

3 cups tomato or V8 juice

1 cup ice water

1–2 teaspoons cayenne pepper

1–2 teaspoons kosher salt

⅓ cup chopped fresh dill, cilantro or basil leaves, for garnish (optional)

½ cup crumbled feta cheese, for garnish (optional)

2 cups Croutons (page 13), for garnish

Place the cucumbers, tomatoes, onion, garlic and peppers in a bowl and toss to combine. Remove half the mixture and place it in a food processor fitted with a steel blade. Pulse 2 or 3 times, until well chopped and combined. Return to the bowl.

Add the olive oil, vinegar, tomato juice, ice water, cayenne and salt, and stir to combine.

Cover and refrigerate at least 2 hours and up to 24 hours. Serve, garnished with the dill, feta and croutons, if desired.

> "Cold soup is a very tricky thing and it is the rare hostess who can carry it off. More often than not the dinner guest is left with the impression that had he only come a little earlier he could have gotten it while it was still hot."
>
> —FRAN LEBOWITZ, JOURNALIST (B. 1951)

Tomato with Cheddar

One of my absolute, all-time favorite soups. The balsamic vinegar in this recipe both cuts the richness and highlights the other flavors. Don't even think of leaving it out.

> "Tart words make no friends; a spoonful of honey will catch more flies than a gallon of vinegar."
>
> —BENJAMIN FRANKLIN, SCIENTIST, STATESMAN AND INVENTOR (1706–1790)

YIELD: ABOUT 12 CUPS

1 tablespoon unsalted butter

1 Spanish onion, halved and chopped

1 carrot, sliced

2 garlic cloves, sliced

Two 28-ounce cans diced or whole tomatoes, including liquid

8 cups Chicken Stock (page 8)

1 cup shredded cheddar cheese

2 tablespoons balsamic vinegar

½ cup heavy or light cream (optional)

½ cup chopped fresh basil leaves, plus additional for garnish

Place a large heavy-bottomed soup pot over medium-high heat and add the butter. When the butter has melted, add the onion, carrot and garlic and cook until tender, 10–15 minutes. Add the tomatoes and chicken stock and bring to a boil. Lower the heat to low and cook until the mixture begins to come together, 30–45 minutes.

Place a small amount in a blender and blend until smooth. Add the cheese and vinegar and repeat, in batches, until all the soup has been blended. Serve immediately, or transfer to a container, cover and refrigerate up to 3 days. Just before serving, stir in the cream, if desired, and the basil. Serve garnished with the extra basil.

Cream of Broccoli

Lauren doesn't even like broccoli, but she begs me to make this soup. If you want to make the soup richer, add 1 cup grated cheddar cheese when you are pureeing it.

This soup should not be frozen.

> "Good manners: The noise you don't make when you're eating soup."
> —BENNETT CERF, EDITOR AND PUBLISHER (1898–1971)

YIELD: ABOUT 18 CUPS

1 tablespoon unsalted butter, olive oil or canola oil
1 Spanish onion, halved and coarsely chopped
1 celery stalk, chopped
2 carrots, thinly sliced
12 cups Chicken Stock (page 8), plus additional if needed
One 3-pound bag broccoli florets
½ cup heavy or light cream (optional)
1-2 teaspoons fresh lemon juice
Kosher salt and black pepper

Place a large heavy-bottomed soup pot over medium heat and when it is hot, add the butter. When the butter has melted, add the onion, celery and carrots and cook until tender, 10–15 minutes.

Add the chicken stock, raise the heat to high and bring to a boil. While the broth is boiling, slowly add the broccoli. Return to a boil briefly.

Lower the heat to medium and cook until the broccoli is just tender, 5–8 minutes.

Remove the solids and place them in a food processor or blender. Process until smooth, gradually adding the hot stock and the cream. Add additional stock if the soup is too thick. Add the lemon juice, season with salt and pepper and serve immediately, or transfer to a container, cover and refrigerate for 1 to 2 days.

Cream of Mushroom

If you like, feel free to substitute more exotic mushrooms, such as portobello, cremini or shiitake, for half of the button mushrooms.

To freeze this soup, puree it but don't add the cream. Reheat gently, adding the cream once the soup is hot.

MUSHROOMS don't take well to being washed; instead, wipe them clean with a damp towel just before cooking.

> "If only one could tell true love from false love as one can tell mushrooms from toadstools."
>
> —KATHERINE MANSFIELD, WRITER (1888–1923)

YIELD: ABOUT 16 CUPS

1 tablespoon unsalted butter

1 Spanish onion, halved and coarsely chopped or sliced

One 40-ounce box button mushrooms, wiped clean with a clean, dry cloth and coarsely chopped, stems included

2 potatoes, unpeeled, diced (about 2 cups) (optional)

12 cups Chicken Stock (page 8)

2 teaspoons dried rosemary

½ cup dry red wine or dry sherry (for a sweeter soup)

1 cup heavy cream

Kosher salt and black pepper

Chopped fresh chives, for garnish (optional)

Freshly grated Parmesan or Gruyère cheese, for garnish (optional)

Place a large heavy-bottomed soup pot over medium heat and when it is hot, add the butter. When the butter has melted, add the onion and cook until tender, 10–15 minutes.

Add the mushrooms and cook until they release their juices, about 15 minutes. Add the potatoes, if using, chicken stock, and rosemary, raise the heat to high and bring to a boil. Lower the heat to low and cook until the potatoes are tender, about 20 minutes.

Remove the solids and place them in a blender or a food processor fitted with a steel blade. Process until completely smooth, gradually adding the hot stock, wine and cream. Season with salt and pepper.

Serve immediately, or transfer to a container, cover, and refrigerate up to 3 days. Garnish with the chives and cheese, if desired.

Mushroom and Sausage Soup

This is a substantial and rustic soup, perfect for a snowy winter evening. Pair it with a baguette and a salad, and maybe a piece of cheese and some fruit, for a satisfying meal.

OREGANO, also called wild marjoram, belongs to the mint family and is related to both marjoram and thyme. Oregano is similar to marjoram but is not as sweet and has a stronger, more pungent flavor and aroma. The word *oregano* is Greek for "joy of the mountain" and was almost unheard of in the United States until soldiers who had been stationed in Italy during World War II returned home raving about it.

YIELD: ABOUT 12 CUPS

(Continued on next page)

2 sweet Italian sausages, taken out of casing

1 Spanish onion, halved and chopped

1 celery stalk, chopped

1 carrot, sliced

½ teaspoon dried oregano

1–1½ pounds (half the 40-ounce box) button mushrooms, coarsely chopped

2 small red new potatoes, sliced

1 teaspoon dried fennel seed

8 cups Chicken Stock (page 8)

1 teaspoon Dijon mustard

¼ teaspoon black pepper

2 scallions, julienned

Place a large heavy-bottomed soup pot over medium-low heat and when it is hot, add the sausage. Cook for 3 minutes, all the while breaking up the sausage with the back of a wooden spoon. Add the onion, celery, carrot and oregano and cook until the vegetables are tender, 10–15 minutes.

Add the mushrooms and cook for an additional 5 minutes.

Add the potatoes, fennel and chicken stock, raise the heat to high and bring to a boil. Lower the heat to low and cook until the potatoes are tender, about 20 minutes.

Remove the solids and place them in a blender or a food processor fitted with a steel blade. Process until smooth, gradually adding the mustard and pepper.

Serve immediately, garnished with the scallions, or transfer to a container, cover and refrigerate overnight.

Minestrone

When you buy a chunk of Parmesan cheese, what do you do with the rind when you're done with the cheese? Here's a reason to buy the cheese *for* the rind: cooking it in the soup adds an almost meaty flavor to this Italian classic.

MAKES 16–20 CUPS

1 tablespoon olive or canola oil
1 Spanish onion, halved and finely chopped
2 garlic cloves, pressed or finely chopped
2 celery stalks, sliced
2 carrots, quartered lengthwise and sliced
2 zucchini, quartered lengthwise and sliced
2 teaspoons dried basil
One 16-ounce can diced tomatoes, drained
10 cups beef or Chicken Stock (page 8)
One 15.5-ounce can red kidney beans, drained and rinsed
1 Parmesan cheese rind (about 5 inches long)
2 cups cooled, cooked medium-size pasta shapes
Kosher salt and black pepper to taste
Freshly grated Parmesan cheese, for garnish
¼ cup chopped fresh basil leaves, for garnish

Place a stockpot over medium heat and when it is hot, add the olive oil. Add the onion, garlic, celery, carrots, zucchini and dried basil and cook, covered, until the vegetables are tender, 10–15 minutes.

Add the tomatoes, stock, beans and Parmesan cheese rind. Raise the heat to high and bring just to a boil. Lower the heat to low and cook, partially covered, for 2 hours.

Transfer to a container, cover and refrigerate at least overnight and up to 2 days.

Remove the Parmesan cheese rind. Place the soup in a pot, add the pasta and gently reheat. Season with salt and pepper. Garnish with Parmesan cheese and fresh basil, and serve.

All-American Beef Chili

This can be served right away (and it's yummy), but it really improves after resting overnight. (Who doesn't?)

In order to eliminate the, um, gastrointestinal distress that often accompanies EATING BEANS, make sure you rinse your beans several times in cold running water. It's the liquid, rather than the beans, that is the culprit.

> "Next to jazz music, there is nothing that lifts the spirit and strengthens the soul more than a good bowl of chili."
> —HARRY JAMES, TRUMPETER AND BAND LEADER (1916–1983)

YIELD: ABOUT 12 CUPS

2 tablespoons vegetable or olive oil

2 Spanish onions, halved and finely chopped

1 red bell pepper, cut into ½-inch pieces

6 garlic cloves, minced or pressed

¼ cup chili powder

1 tablespoon ground cumin

1 teaspoon crushed red pepper flakes, or more to taste

1 teaspoon dried oregano

½ teaspoon cayenne pepper, or more to taste

2½ pounds ground beef or ground turkey

3–4 chipotle chiles in adobo, chopped (page 184)

Two 16-ounce cans dark red kidney or black beans, drained and rinsed

One 28-ounce can diced tomatoes, undrained

One 28-ounce can tomato puree

2 limes, cut into wedges

Optional garnishes:

Diced fresh tomatoes
Diced avocado
Sliced scallions
Chopped red onion
Chopped fresh cilantro leaves
Sour cream
Shredded Monterey Jack or cheddar cheese
Chopped jalapeño chiles

Place a large heavy-bottomed nonreactive Dutch oven over medium heat and when it is hot, add the vegetable oil. Add the onions, bell pepper and garlic and cook, stirring occasionally, until tender, 10–15 minutes. Add the chili powder, cumin, red pepper flakes, oregano and cayenne and cook, stirring constantly, until well combined, about 2 minutes. Raise the heat to medium-high. Add half the beef and cook, breaking up the pieces with a wooden spoon, until it is just beginning to brown, 3–4 minutes.

Add the chipotle chiles, 1 tablespoon of the adobo sauce (or more to taste) and the remaining beef. Cook again until the beef browns, 3–4 minutes. Add the beans, tomatoes and tomato puree and bring to a boil. Lower the heat to low and simmer, partially covered, stirring occasionally, for 1 hour.

Remove the cover and cook, stirring occasionally, until the beef is tender and the chili is dark, rich and slightly thickened, about 1 hour longer. If the chili gets too thick, add ½ cup water.

Serve immediately, garnished with lime wedges and the other garnishes, if desired, or cover and refrigerate up to 5 days or freeze up to 1 month.

White Chili

This lighter chili is a welcome change from (and cooks more quickly than) the traditional version. Be sure to pass lots of accompaniments so that diners can garnish to their own taste.

CANNELLINI BEANS are large white kidney beans. Other white beans, like white navy and Great Northern, can be substituted.

> "It doesn't take much to see that the problems of three little people doesn't add up to a hill of beans in this crazy world. Someday you'll understand that. Now, now ... Here's looking at you, kid."
> —HUMPHREY BOGART, IN *CASABLANCA*

YIELD: ABOUT 12 CUPS

1 tablespoon olive oil

2 Spanish onions, halved and chopped

5 garlic cloves, minced

1 tablespoon chili powder

2 teaspoons ground cumin

2 teaspoons dried oregano

2 teaspoons crushed red pepper flakes

3 pounds ground turkey or chicken

Four 16-ounce cans cannellini beans, drained and rinsed

2 cups water or Chicken Stock (page 8)

½ cup heavy cream

Kosher salt

Optional garnishes:

Lemon or lime quarters
Fresh cilantro leaves
Salsa
Grated cheddar cheese
Sour cream

Place a large heavy-bottomed soup pot over medium heat and when it is hot, add the olive oil. Add the onions and garlic and cook until they are lightly golden, 5–7 minutes. Add the chili powder, cumin, oregano and red pepper flakes and cook for 2 minutes. Add the turkey and cook, breaking it up with the back of a wooden spoon, until white, 4–5 minutes. Add the beans, water and cream and cook for 5 minutes. Lower the heat to low and cook until the chili comes together, about 20 minutes. Add salt to taste.

Serve immediately, garnished with lemon wedges, if desired; pass any other garnishes. Or the chili can be covered and refrigerated up to 5 days or frozen up to 1 month.

Bouillabaisse with Rouille

This is an uncharacteristically long list of ingredients (for me), but please don't be alarmed and turn the page. This traditional French fisherman's stew is well worth making for an informal dinner party once or twice a year. It is best made one day ahead (which saves lots of time the day of your party); add the fish just prior to serving. Serve it with the rouille, baguettes and a salad. A plate of cheese and fruit, or a fruit tart, would be a perfect finish.

> "Bouillabaisse is one of those classic dishes whose glory has encircled the world, and the miracle consists of this: there are as many Bouillabaisses as there are good chefs.... Each brings to his own version his special touch."
> —CURNONSKY (MAURICE EDMOND SAILLAND), FRENCH WRITER
> AND GASTRONOME (1872–1956)

ROUILLE is a traditional French sauce, similar in texture to a mayonnaise, made with either bell or chile peppers, garlic and bread crumbs. It is usually served with fish stews.

PERNOD and ANISETTE are both sweet licorice-flavored liqueurs, and while SAMBUCA is less sweet, they are all interchangeable for this recipe.

Heady and aromatic, SAFFRON comes as a powder and as the more preferable threads, which should be crushed just prior to using. Saffron is the dried stigmas of the crocus flower. One flower holds only three stigmas, each of which must be picked by hand. It is not surprising then that saffron is the world's most expensive and precious spice (by weight, not by use), since it takes 75,000 flowers to produce 1 pound of saffron threads. Many people wonder if saffron is all that it's cracked up to be—if it really adds flavor to a dish. It does. Bouillabaisse, along with paella and risotto Milanese, are its best illustrations.

SERVES 10

For the bouillabaisse:

2 tablespoons olive oil

2 Spanish onions, halved and chopped

4 garlic cloves, minced

1–2 fennel bulbs, diced

3 carrots, chopped

2 celery stalks, chopped

Two 16-ounce cans diced tomatoes, undrained

Zest of 1/2 orange, cut in thin julienne

2 bay leaves

1 teaspoon dried thyme

2–3 teaspoons fennel seed

2 cups diced potatoes

4 cups Chicken Stock (page 8)

4 cups fish broth, or 2 cups clam juice and 2 cups water

Pinch saffron, or more to taste

4 tablespoons Pernod, Anisette or Sambuca

1 pound lean fish, such as cod, monkfish or halibut, cut in big chunks

2 pounds mussels, cleaned and debearded

1/2 pound scallops, quartered

1 pound shrimp (any size is fine), peeled and deveined

1/4 cup chopped fresh basil leaves, for garnish

1/4 cup chopped fresh Italian flat-leaf parsley leaves, for garnish

1 tablespoon fresh thyme leaves, for garnish

(Continued on next page)

For the rouille:

1 roasted red bell pepper (page 13)
2 garlic cloves
1 slice white bread
1 tablespoon warm water
½ cup olive oil
½ teaspoon kosher salt
¼ teaspoon cayenne pepper

TO MAKE THE BOUILLABAISSE: Place a large, heavy bottomed pot (such as a Dutch oven) over medium heat and when it is hot, add the olive oil. Add the onions, garlic, fennel, carrots and celery and cook, stirring occasionally, until tender, 10–15 minutes.

Add the tomatoes, orange zest, bay leaves, thyme, fennel seed and potatoes and cook for 5 minutes. Raise the heat to medium-high, add the chicken stock, fish broth, saffron and 2 tablespoons Pernod and cook for 5 minutes. Lower the heat to low and cook until the stew has come together and reduced somewhat, about 1 hour. If you are cooking this a day ahead, cover and refrigerate. Otherwise, add the fish, mussels, scallops and shrimp, cover and cook until the fish is cooked through, about 10 minutes. If you are refrigerating, just prior to serving, gently reheat over low heat and then add the fish.

While the bouillabaisse is cooking, and just prior to serving, PREPARE THE ROUILLE: Place the bell pepper, garlic and bread in a food processor fitted with a steel blade and process until well chopped. Add the water and pulse to combine. While the machine is running, gradually add the olive oil, salt and cayenne pepper, and mix until thick and well blended. Set aside.

Just prior to serving, add the remaining 2 tablespoons Pernod to the bouillabaisse. Transfer to heated shallow bowls, and garnish each bowl with the parsley, basil and thyme leaves and a big dollop of rouille. Serve immediately.

Sandwiches

These aren't really recipes, but rather ideas for sandwiches. The possibilities, as with soup, are endless. It is the one meal that I am happy to scrounge around for in the fridge. In fact some of the best combinations are the result of happenstance: simply seeing some olive paste, a chunk of cheddar cheese or some lonely leaves of radicchio has inspired me to make new matches. Although I don't eat sandwiches very often, there is nothing quite like a really good one. As a rule, I put about 3 to 4 ounces of meat on meat sandwiches, and about 1 to 2 ounces of cheese, but my favorite part tends to be what's on the rest of the sandwich. For me it's about the "stuff." Use these only as guidelines and experiment endlessly: try chutneys, salsa, flavored mayonnaises, barbecue sauce, julienned carrots, baby tomatoes . . . the list goes on and on.

Turkey, avocado and bacon

Turkey, stuffing and cranberry sauce or chutney

Turkey, Brie cheese and curried mayonnaise

Turkey, hummus, pesto, avocado, cucumber and tomatoes

Fresh tomatoes, mozzarella and fresh basil

k steak (pages 196–200)

e 194) with ketchup, barbecue sauce or chutney

heddar cheese

h or without goat cheese, mozzarella or Brie cheese

th pesto

dar with chutney (pages 23, 175)

with mustard or olive oil

pesto, with or without tomatoes

page 10) and cream cheese

(page 28), with or without cheese

ge 13) and mozzarella, with or without pesto

rs or apples

d tomatoes

unded) (page 135) and mustard

butter

nnaise

8) and cheddar cheese

d cream cheese with red onion

anas and honey

tomato

ADD-ONS TO ALMOST ANY SANDWICH

Carrot ribbons (cut with a potato peeler)

Cucumbers, thinly sliced

Radishes, thinly sliced

Apples or pears, thinly sliced

Fresh basil leaves

Chopped nuts

Tomatoes

Any greens

Salad Dressings and Salads

"To make a good salad is to be a brilliant diplomatist—the problem is entirely the same in both cases. To know how much oil one must mix with one's vinegar."

—OSCAR WILDE, DRAMATIST, NOVELIST AND POET (1854–1900)

I like salads to be either very, very simple, consisting of mostly greens (one kind or many different, such as mesclun) drizzled with a vinaigrette, or very complex, a variety of greens with tons of different ingredients. In general, salads should be composed of contrasting flavors, mild with strong (iceberg lettuce with blue cheese), crunchy with soft (green beans with mushrooms), raw with cooked (romaine lettuce and croutons) and sweet with bitter or salty (peaches and feta cheese with mesclun).

More complex salads are composed of several different lettuces (romaine, radicchio, watercress, endive and arugula are a great combination), several different vegetables, meats, fish, cheeses, even fresh fruit, dried fruit and nuts. Almost nothing is inappropriate in a salad.

It's a rare dinner in my house that doesn't include salad, so I like to have lots of dressings on hand. Although Balsamic (page 67) and Caesar (page 71) are the most commonly consumed and most beloved by my children, having many options to choose from can definitely make eating salad an easy and simple choice (especially if you buy mesclun).

The salad dressings, as well as some of the salads, here are updated versions of some classics. While I've certainly been known to eat Curried Chicken Salad (page 84) and Cobb Salad (page 86) during a snowstorm, they're really designed for lunch and simple summer dinners.

Balsamic Vinaigrette

I started making this dressing about twenty-five years ago, and although it's easy to make as needed, it's heavenly to have some in the fridge at all times (especially since Lauren, my fourteen-year-old daughter, slathers it on almost anything edible). An all-purpose vinaigrette that's great drizzled on any green or vegetable, it's also good on grilled tuna or chicken or used as a marinade for chicken and steak.

Balsamic Vinaigrette is a perfect dressing for a salad of chopped romaine lettuce, blue cheese, pear and pecans; or mesclun greens with grape or cherry tomatoes, red onion and goat cheese; or romaine with green beans, tomatoes, feta or blue cheese and radishes. Try it also on halved avocadoes, alone or on a scoop of tuna (page 80).

Since BALSAMIC VINEGAR is made from grape juice, it's not really that surprising that it is so appealing. Aged in oak, ash, cherry, mulberry and juniper barrels for eight to twelve years, basalmic vinegar is sweet, rich and tart-sour. It imparts an indefinable quality to everything it's included in.

YIELD: ABOUT 2 CUPS

4 garlic cloves, chopped (optional)
2 teaspoons Dijon mustard
¾ cup balsamic vinegar
1 cup extra-virgin olive oil
1 teaspoon kosher salt
Black pepper to taste

Place the garlic, if using, mustard and vinegar in a blender or a food processor fitted with a steel blade and process until thoroughly combined. While the machine is running, gradually add the olive oil. Add the salt, and pepper to taste. Transfer to a glass container, cover and refrigerate up to 1 month. If the oil separates from the vinegar, shake the container vigorously. If it solidifies, leave it out at room temperature for a few minutes and then shake well.

Lemon Pepper Dressing

This tart and lively dressing can be used on salads and steamed vegetables (especially artichokes and broccoli), and drizzled on grilled chicken, salmon or swordfish. Pepper lovers might want to increase the amount of one or both of the peppers (keeping in mind that the heat of the peppers strengthens as they sit). And of course, the pepper can be decreased or simply eliminated.

Good matches for this dressing include a salad of romaine, tomatoes, bell pepper, feta cheese, olives and onion; or salad greens with leftover flank steak, marinated artichoke hearts, blue cheese, red onion and pistachios or walnuts.

> "I don't know when pepper mills in a restaurant got to be right behind frankincense and myrrh in prominence. It used to be in a little jar that sat next to the salt on the table and everyone passed it around, sneezed, and it was no big deal."
>
> —ERMA BOMBECK, HUMORIST (1927–1996)

YIELD: ABOUT 3 CUPS

1 cup fresh lemon juice
2 cups extra-virgin olive oil
1½ teaspoons black pepper
1½ teaspoons crushed red pepper flakes
2 teaspoons kosher salt

Place all the ingredients in a small bowl and whisk until emulsified. Transfer to a glass container, cover and refrigerate up to 2 weeks. If the oil separates from the lemon juice, vigorously shake the container. If it solidifies, leave it out at room temperature for a few minutes and then shake well.

Curried Dressing

Although this dressing is highly flavored, it complements many different flavors. It's especially good on a salad of bunch spinach, apples or pears, sesame seeds and raisins or dried cranberries, or on romaine with cheddar cheese, apples and walnuts. It can also be used as a marinade for chicken or a drizzle for grilled salmon.

CHUTNEY is a surprisingly versatile Indian condiment made of fruit, spices, an acid and sugar. It ranges from smooth to chunky and mild to hot. Chutney is most often made with mangoes but there are also delicious chutneys made with peaches, apricots, cranberries and bananas.

> "According to the Spanish proverb, four persons are wanted to make a good salad: a spendthrift (for oil), a miser for vinegar, a counselor for salt and a madman to stir it all up."
>
> —JOHN GERARD, JESUIT PRIEST (1564–1637)

· YIELD: ABOUT 2 CUPS

1 cup white wine vinegar

1 cup olive oil

2 tablespoons mango chutney, store-bought or homemade (page 23)

2 teaspoons curry powder

2 teaspoons dry mustard

2 teaspoons kosher salt

½ teaspoon Tabasco sauce

Place all the ingredients in a blender and blend until smooth. Transfer to a glass container, cover and refrigerate up to 3 weeks. If the oil separates from the vinegar, vigorously shake the container. If it solidifies, leave it out at room temperature for a few minutes and then shake well.

Pesto Dressing

When my friend Nancy served this dressing on a simple green salad for family and friends, everyone loved it but no one could guess what was in it. Pal Urit Chaimovitz guessed artichoke hearts and Nancy's husband, Steve, said honey. But it was seven-year-old Joey who put his nose toward the salad and correctly guessed pesto. While it's great on any combination of mixed greens, it's also perfect drizzled on tomatoes and goat cheese, chilled new potatoes, cold noodles with julienned vegetables, and pasta with halved grape or cherry tomatoes and fresh mozzarella or Parmesan cheese.

YIELD: ABOUT 2 CUPS

¼ cup prepared pesto
1 cup extra-virgin olive oil
1 cup fresh lemon juice or red wine vinegar
1 teaspoon kosher salt
¼ teaspoon black pepper

Place all the ingredients in a small bowl and whisk until emulsified. Transfer to a glass container, cover and refrigerate up to 2 weeks. If the oil separates from the lemon juice or vinegar, simply shake the container well. If it solidifies, leave it out at room temperature for a few minutes and then shake well.

Caesar Salad Dressing

While this is the traditional dressing for a classic Caesar Salad—whole or chopped romaine lettuce, lots of Parmesan cheese (optional in the dressing but not in the salad itself) and croutons—you can use it as an all-purpose salad dressing. There is some debate as to whether the original version contained anchovies. If you don't like anchovies, don't avoid this dressing—just leave them out. You can substitute feta cheese for the Parmesan in the salad and for a main course, add cooked chicken, shrimp or steak.

Tiny silvery fish with blue-green backs, ANCHOVIES are most often filleted, salt-cured and canned in oil. Typically sold flat or rolled in flat tins, they are rich in omega-3 oils, calcium and iron. If they're too salty for your taste, soak them in cold water for half an hour. Once you open a tin of anchovies, transfer them to a glass container and refrigerate; do not continue using the tin.

YIELD: ABOUT 2½ CUPS

4–5 garlic cloves, sliced
3–4 anchovy fillets
2 teaspoons Dijon mustard
1 cup fresh lemon juice
1½ cups olive oil
2 teaspoons kosher salt
1 teaspoon black pepper
¼ cup freshly grated Parmesan cheese (optional)

Place the garlic and anchovies in a blender or a food processor fitted with a steel blade and process until they are well chopped. Add the remaining ingredients and blend until the dressing is emulsified. Transfer to a glass container, cover and refrigerate up to 1 month. If the oil separates from the lemon juice, simply shake the container well. If it solidifies, leave it out at room temperature for a few minutes and then shake well.

Green Goddess Dressing

Legend has it that Green Goddess Dressing was created in the 1920s by the chef at San Francisco's Palace Hotel in honor of actor George Arliss, who was appearing in a play called *The Green Goddess.* It is said that he requested that a dressing be named after him, but why this particular combination became Green Goddess is a mystery to me.

Thick, creamy and slightly biting, Green Goddess is great on almost any green leaf or vegetable, but I especially like it on quarters of iceberg lettuce, cucumber cubes, tomatoes and bacon; a salad of romaine lettuce, tomatoes, red onion and walnuts or pecans; or on lightly steamed asparagus or artichokes. It's also wonderful dolloped on grilled, broiled or steamed fish, especially grilled tuna or salmon, and on grilled burgers.

YIELD: ABOUT 1½ CUPS

2 garlic cloves, sliced

2 anchovy fillets

3 scallions

1 cup fresh Italian flat-leaf parsley leaves

1½ teaspoons dried tarragon

¼ cup sour cream or full-fat plain yogurt

¼ cup buttermilk

¼ cup mayonnaise

2 tablespoons white (distilled) vinegar

½–1 teaspoon black pepper

Place the garlic, anchovies, scallions, parsley and tarragon in a blender or a food processor fitted with a steel blade and process until smooth. Add the sour cream and buttermilk and blend until smooth. Transfer to a glass container, add the mayonnaise, vinegar and pepper, and mix by hand to combine. Cover and refrigerate up to 1 week. If the dressing separates, simply shake the container well.

Blue Cheese Dressing

Thick and creamy, this can be used as a dip for crudités or Boston Trio chicken (page 129) as well as a dressing on any green salad. A slightly updated but classic combo for this dressing is a wedge of iceberg lettuce sprinkled with bacon, avocado and cherry or grape tomatoes. Another impressive salad combination is romaine lettuce with pears and lightly toasted walnuts. Burgers and roast beef sandwiches also benefit from this tangy combination, as do steamed broccoli and cauliflower.

BUTTERMILK adds a certain ineffable tang; its clear, almost acidic taste is a perfect partner for blue cheese. However, the name is confusing since there is no butter in buttermilk. Originally, when fresh milk was allowed to stand, the lightweight butterfat globules rose to the top, forming cream, which was then churned into butter. What remained at the bottom was skim milk, which when affected by the airborne bacteria is converted into buttermilk. The buttermilk you buy today is a cultured product like yogurt, inspired by, but not exactly duplicating, the flavor of the original.

YIELD: ABOUT 3 CUPS

1½ cups crumbled blue cheese
2 cups buttermilk or full-fat plain yogurt
1 teaspoon finely chopped garlic (optional)
2 teaspoons fresh lemon juice
1 teaspoon kosher salt
¼–½ teaspoon black pepper

Place the blue cheese in a bowl and mash with a fork until it is crumbly but not completely creamy. Add the buttermilk and continue mashing. Add the garlic, if desired, and lemon juice and mix to combine. Add the salt and pepper. Transfer to a glass container, cover and refrigerate at least 4 hours and up to 1 week. If the dressing separates, simply shake the container well.

Thousand Island/Russian Dressing

For me, Thousand Island and Russian dressings are interchangeable, as they have as their chief components both mayonnaise and chili sauce. The name "Russian dressing" is really a misnomer because it's come to be as American as apple pie. One rumor has it that the name derives from the fact that it originally had Russian caviar in it. Today, horseradish or relish often gives the dressing its texture.

Thousand Island Dressing originated in the Thousand Islands area in upstate New York. The owner of a restaurant there fed it to an actress who told a friend who told a friend who told a friend, and the rest is history.

Whatever you call it, it's ideal on roast beef sandwiches and turkey club sandwiches, on greens, and on wedges of iceberg lettuce with chopped bacon.

Contrary to common opinion, prepared CHILI SAUCE is not necessarily spicy. Generally it is a mixture of tomatoes and chile peppers that have been cooked together and then pureed with vinegar, sugar, onions, and various other seasonings (depending on the brand). The sauce obtains its spiciness, or lack thereof, from the chile peppers. There are three traditional prepared chili sauces: Thai, Vietnamese and American. Typically the Thai and Vietnamese contain extremely hot chile peppers, while the American variety is generally milder.

YIELD: ABOUT 1½ CUPS

1 cup mayonnaise
⅓ cup chili sauce
1 tablespoon prepared horseradish
1 tablespoon Worcestershire sauce
1 tablespoon fresh lemon juice

Place everything in a small bowl and mix to combine. Transfer to a glass container, cover and refrigerate up to 1 week. If the dressing separates, simply shake the container well.

Greek Salad with Romaine

This variation on the classic Greek salad includes avocadoes and bell peppers.

SERVES 4

1 head romaine lettuce, dark leaves discarded, the rest torn

2 English cucumbers, cubed

2 ripe tomatoes, cubed

1 red, orange or yellow bell pepper, diced

¼ cup black olives, Kalamata preferred

1 ripe avocado, cubed (optional)

½ pound feta cheese, crumbled

2 tablespoons chopped fresh mint leaves (optional)

1 tablespoon chopped fresh oregano or 1 teaspoon dried oregano

1–2 garlic cloves, finely chopped

¼ cup olive oil

¼ cup fresh lemon juice (about 1 lemon)

Place the lettuce, cucumbers, tomatoes, bell pepper and black olives in a large serving bowl. Add the avocado, if desired, and sprinkle with the cheese, mint, if desired, and oregano.

Place the garlic, olive oil and lemon juice in a small bowl and whisk together. Drizzle over the salad and serve immediately.

Annette's Corn Salad

When my sister-in-law, Annette, told me about this summer salad, I turned my nose up. But she didn't warn me how truly amazing it was and that I would be happy to spend a good deal of my summer shucking and shaving corn. If you must, you can use frozen or canned corn, but I wouldn't recommend it.

> "To get the best results, you must talk to your vegetables."
> —CHARLES, PRINCE OF WALES (B. 1948)

YIELD: ABOUT 5–6 CUPS; SERVES 4–6

For the salad:

2 cups fresh corn kernels

One 15.5-ounce can red kidney or black beans, rinsed and drained

1 cup chopped seeded plum tomatoes

¼ cup chopped red onion

¼ cup chopped fresh basil leaves

For the dressing:

2 tablespoons olive oil

2 tablespoons fresh lemon or lime juice

¼ cup chopped fresh cilantro leaves

2 large garlic cloves, crushed or minced

¼ teaspoon crushed red pepper flakes (optional)

½–1 teaspoon kosher salt

TO MAKE THE SALAD: Place all the ingredients in a medium-size bowl and toss to mix.
TO MAKE THE DRESSING: Place all the ingredients in a small bowl and whisk well.
Add the dressing to the corn mixture, cover and refrigerate at least 2 hours and up to overnight. Serve chilled or at room temperature.

Tuscan Bread Salad

This is an ingenious—and delicious—use for day-old bread.

I prefer ENGLISH CUCUMBERS to the more familiar, squatter, supermarket variety. Although slightly more expensive, they taste better and are never bitter. They do not need to be peeled or seeded, thus saving time.

SERVES 4–6

2 cups day-old Italian or French bread cubes
2 medium tomatoes, diced
1 English cucumber, halved and thinly sliced
1 red onion, halved and diced
1 red, orange or yellow bell pepper, diced
¼ cup coarsely chopped fresh basil leaves
1 tablespoon finely chopped fresh oregano leaves
½ cup coarsely chopped fresh Italian flat-leaf parsley leaves
2 garlic cloves, finely chopped or pressed
2 tablespoons red wine vinegar
2 tablespoons olive oil
½ teaspoon kosher salt
¼ teaspoon black pepper

Place the bread, vegetables and herbs in a large mixing bowl and toss to mix.

Place the garlic, vinegar, olive oil, salt and pepper in a bowl and mix well. Drizzle the dressing over the vegetables, cover and refrigerate at least 1 hour and up to 4 hours.

Mustard Potato Salad

This tangy version of an American classic will be a welcome addition to any picnic or barbecue.

ITALIAN FLAT-LEAF PARSLEY is slightly peppery, darker in color and stronger in flavor than curly-leaf parsley but less bitter. Once I discovered it, I never went back to curly-leaf. The best way to store parsley is to wash it, shake off the excess water, wrap it in a paper towel and place it in a plastic bag in the vegetable drawer. Never substitute dried parsley, a totally worthless purchase.

> "Peace of mind and a comfortable income are predicted by a dream of eating potatoes in any form."
>
> —NED BALLANTYNE AND STELLA COELI (FROM 1940)

SERVES 6–8

3 pounds new potatoes, peeled if desired, quartered or halved

¼ cup low- or full-fat plain yogurt

¼ cup mayonnaise

¼ cup Dijon mustard

¼ cup sour cream

3–4 celery stalks, julienned

3–4 carrots, julienned

4 scallions, chopped

1 cup finely chopped fresh Italian flat-leaf parsley leaves

Kosher salt and black pepper to taste

Place the potatoes in a large stockpot and cover with cold water. Bring to a boil and cook until the potatoes are tender, 15–20 minutes. Drain and transfer to a large bowl to cool to room temperature.

While the potatoes are cooling, place the yogurt, mayonnaise, mustard and sour cream in a small bowl and mix well.

When the potatoes have cooled, add the yogurt mixture and the celery, carrots, scallions and parsley, and gently mix. Season with salt and pepper. Serve immediately, or cover and refrigerate up to overnight.

Curried Potato Salad

A vaguely Indian and very tasty variation, this potato salad goes particularly well with grilled chicken or lamb.

> "What I say is that, if a fellow really likes potatoes, he must be a pretty decent sort of fellow." —A.A. MILNE, WRITER (1882–1956)

SERVES 6–8

3 pounds new potatoes, peeled if desired, quartered or halved

1 cup mayonnaise

⅓ cup sour cream or full-fat plain yogurt

2 tablespoons curry powder

¾ cup fresh green peas

5 scallions, finely chopped

⅓ cup chopped fresh cilantro leaves

2 teaspoons kosher salt

1 teaspoon black pepper

Place the potatoes in a large stockpot and cover with cold water. Bring to a boil and cook until the potatoes are tender, 15–20 minutes. Drain and transfer to a large bowl to cool to room temperature.

While the potatoes are cooling, place the mayonnaise, sour cream and curry powder in a small bowl and mix well.

When the potatoes have cooled, add the mayonnaise mixture and the remaining ingredients and stir until well coated. Serve immediately, or cover and refrigerate up to overnight.

Classic Tuna Salad

Great stuffed into avocado or tomato halves, or mounded on a bed of lettuce.

> "I refuse to believe that trading recipes is silly. Tunafish casserole is at least as real as corporate stock."
> —BARBARA GRIZZUTI HARRISON, WRITER (1934–2002)

SERVES 3–4

Two 6-ounce cans white albacore tuna packed in water,
    drained and flaked with a fork
2 heaping tablespoons mayonnaise
2 tablespoons fresh lemon juice
2 teaspoons Dijon mustard
1 celery stalk, finely chopped
¼ small red onion, finely chopped
Kosher salt and black pepper

Place the tuna, mayonnaise, lemon juice, mustard, celery and onion in a medium-size bowl and mix to combine. Add salt and pepper to taste. Cover and refrigerate at least 1 hour and up to overnight.

Curried Tuna

A little tart, a little sweet and a lot of savory, this is not your mother's tuna salad.

> "It is more fun to talk with someone who doesn't use long, difficult words but rather short, easy words like 'What about lunch?'"
>
> —A. A. MILNE, WRITER (1882–1956)

SERVES 3–4

Two 6-ounce cans white albacore tuna packed in water,
    drained and flaked with a fork
2 heaping tablespoons mayonnaise
2 tablespoons fresh lemon juice
2 teaspoons Dijon mustard
1 celery stalk, finely chopped
¼ small red onion, finely chopped
1 tablespoon curry powder
1 tablespoon chutney (any kind is fine)
Kosher salt and black pepper
1 tart apple, such as Granny Smith, unpeeled, diced
1–2 tablespoons chopped fresh cilantro leaves, plus additional for garnish

Place the tuna, mayonnaise, lemon juice, mustard, celery, onion, curry powder and chutney in a medium-size bowl and mix to combine. Add salt and pepper to taste. Cover and refrigerate at least 1 hour and up to overnight.

Just prior to serving, stir in the apple and cilantro. Garnish with the extra cilantro.

Mediterranean Tuna

Originally from France, black olive paste is more commonly known as *tapenade,* and is a puree of black olives, capers, garlic, anchovies and olive oil. It is often used as a spread for crackers. Here it infuses a simple tuna salad with the flavors of the South of France.

SERVES 3–4

Two 6-ounce cans white albacore tuna packed in water,
    drained and flaked with a fork
2 heaping tablespoons mayonnaise
2 tablespoons fresh lemon juice
2 teaspoons Dijon mustard
1 celery stalk, finely chopped
¼ small red onion, finely chopped
¼ cup diced roasted red bell pepper (page 13)
1 heaping tablespoon black olive paste or 2 tablespoons finely
    chopped Kalamata olives
2 tablespoons capers, drained and chopped
2 anchovy fillets, minced
1–2 tablespoons chopped fresh Italian flat-leaf parsley leaves
Kosher salt and black pepper to taste

Place all the ingredients in a medium-size bowl and mix to combine. Cover and refrigerate at least 1 hour and up to overnight.

Salad Niçoise

A perfect lunchtime salad. *Niçoise* means "as prepared in Nice"—in other words, a salad that includes ingredients found on the French Riviera.

SERVES 4

For the dressing:

1 garlic clove, minced

2 teaspoons Dijon mustard

2 tablespoons white wine vinegar

¼ cup olive oil

1 teaspoon kosher salt

½ teaspoon black pepper

For the salad:

Two 6-ounce cans white albacore tuna packed in water,
    drained and flaked with a fork

1 red, orange or yellow bell pepper, diced

2–3 anchovy fillets, minced

12–14 black French Niçoise or black Greek olives, coarsely chopped

1 cup grape tomatoes

1 cup green beans, halved

4–6 new potatoes, cooked, cooled and cut into quarters or eighths

2 scallions, chopped

4 cups mesclun greens

2–3 hard-cooked eggs, sliced, for garnish (optional)

TO MAKE THE DRESSING: Place all the ingredients in a small bowl and whisk until completely combined. Set aside.

TO MAKE THE SALAD: Place all the ingredients except the mesclun and eggs in a large bowl and very gently mix to combine. Or arrange them decoratively and do not combine the ingredients. Divide the mesclun among four plates. Pour the dressing over the salad and if serving the mixed version, gently toss.

Divide the salad among the four plates and serve immediately, garnished with the eggs, if desired.

Curried Chicken Salad

Sweet and spicy, this is a more interesting variation of the classic recipe.

TO POACH CHICKEN, place 1¾ pounds raw chicken in a deep skillet or saucepan, cover with cold water (about 4 cups), and bring to a boil over high heat. Lower the heat and cook for 10 minutes. Off heat, turn the chicken pieces over and set aside for 20 minutes. Remove the breasts with a slotted spoon and proceed with the recipe, or transfer to a container or a resealable plastic bag, cover or seal, and refrigerate up to overnight.

This quantity of chicken makes 3¾–4 cups shredded. If you want to cook more chicken, either use a larger pot or reuse the poaching liquid (in the same day). Do not substitute this poaching liquid for chicken stock: it lacks the necessary depth and flavor.

YIELD: ABOUT 4½ CUPS; SERVES 4–6

¼ cup mayonnaise
3 tablespoons mango chutney, store-bought or homemade (page 23)
1 tablespoon curry powder
1½ pounds poached chicken, torn into shreds or diced
2 celery stalks, diced or sliced
1 apple, peach or mango, diced
¼ cup chopped fresh cilantro or basil leaves, or a combination,
    plus additional for garnish

Place the mayonnaise, chutney and curry powder in a medium-size bowl and mix well.

Add the remaining ingredients and mix to combine. Cover and refrigerate at least 1 hour and up to overnight. Just prior to serving, garnish with the extra cilantro and/or basil.

Cilantro Chicken Salad

Inspired by Asian flavors, this fresh tasting chicken salad is made without mayonnaise.

Pressed from sesame seeds, TOASTED SESAME OIL is smoky and nutty and should be used in very small amounts or it will overwhelm a dish.

> "Love, like a chicken salad or restaurant hash, must be taken with blind faith or it loses its flavor."
> —HELEN ROWLAND, JOURNALIST (1876–1950)

YIELD: ABOUT 4½ CUPS

1 garlic clove, minced

2½ tablespoons chopped fresh cilantro leaves

2½ tablespoons rice vinegar

2½ tablespoons canola oil

½ teaspoon toasted sesame oil

Grated zest and juice of 1 lime

¼ teaspoon kosher salt

1½ pounds poached chicken (page 84), torn into shreds or diced

2 tablespoons chopped scallion greens

½ teaspoon Vietnamese chili garlic sauce

½ English cucumber, julienned

½ red bell pepper, julienned

Place the garlic, cilantro, vinegar, oils, lime zest and juice, and salt in a medium-size bowl and mix well.

Add the remaining ingredients and mix to combine. Cover and refrigerate at least 1 hour and up to 4 hours.

Cobb Salad

Packed full of protein and fat, Cobb Salad seems to me the perfect fare for anyone on a low-carbohydrate diet. In 1936, so the story goes, Bob Cobb, the owner of the Brown Derby restaurant in Los Angeles, went into the restaurant's kitchen and put whatever intrigued him into a salad. He served it to some friends, who later came back looking to have it replicated.

Bob Cobb would probably approve of any or all of the following: substitute feta for the blue cheese, prosciutto for the bacon or steak for the chicken.

> "I don't like food that's too carefully arranged; it makes me think that the chef is spending too much time arranging and not enough time cooking. If I wanted a picture I'd buy a painting."
>
> —ANDY ROONEY, JOURNALIST AND TV COMMENTATOR (B. 1919)

SERVES 4

For the salad:

1 pound poached chicken (page 84) or cooked turkey breast, shredded

½ pound bacon, cooked, blotted with a paper towel, and chopped

1–2 avocadoes, cubed

3 large tomatoes, cubed

¼ pound blue cheese, well crumbled

¼ cup chopped fresh chives

2 large hard-cooked eggs, chilled if desired, and halved or quartered

2–3 cups chopped romaine lettuce

2–3 cups watercress leaves

For the dressing:

¼ cup olive oil
2 tablespoons red wine vinegar
2 tablespoons balsamic vinegar
2 teaspoons Dijon mustard
2 garlic cloves, minced
¼ teaspoon Worcestershire sauce
1 teaspoon black pepper

TO MAKE THE SALAD: Place all the salad ingredients except the lettuce and watercress in a large mixing bowl. Pour the dressing over the salad and gently toss.

Divide the romaine and watercress evenly among 4 plates and top with equal amounts of chicken salad. Serve immediately.

TO MAKE THE DRESSING: Place all the dressing ingredients in a blender and blend until smooth. Set aside.

Lemon Tarragon Chicken Salad

Before I started writing cookbooks I owned From the Night Kitchen, a take-out shop in Brookline Village, Massachusetts. One couple came in every time they were going to take a trip (and they traveled a lot). They would have me pack a lunch for the plane that always included this salad. I always think of them when I fly and when I make this salad. They would certainly have agreed with Wolfgang Puck, chef and restaurateur, who said, "To me, an airplane is a great place to diet." Unless of course you bring your own lunch.

> "Ask not what you can do for your country. Ask what's for lunch."
> —ORSON WELLES, ACTOR, DIRECTOR, SCREENWRITER (1915–1985)

The most intense lemon flavor comes from the LEMON ZEST (the outermost layer of the rind). An average lemon supplies about 1 tablespoon grated zest and 3–4 table-spoons juice.

YIELD: ABOUT 4½ CUPS; SERVES 4–6

5 tablespoons mayonnaise

5 tablespoons full-fat plain yogurt or sour cream

¼ cup chopped fresh Italian flat-leaf parsley leaves

1½ teaspoons dried tarragon

1½ pounds poached chicken (page 84), torn into shreds or diced

½ tart apple, peeled if desired, and diced

6 dried apricots, chopped

¼ cup finely chopped, lightly toasted pecans, walnuts or almonds (page 12)

1 teaspoon freshly grated lemon zest

½ teaspoon kosher salt

Place the mayonnaise, yogurt, parsley and tarragon in a medium-size bowl and mix well.

Add the remaining ingredients and mix to combine. Cover and refrigerate at least 1 hour and up to overnight.

Sides

"A fanatic is always the fellow on the opposite side."

—WILL ROGERS, HUMORIST (1879–1935)

Like most modern-day parents balancing work and family, I try to make dinner a relatively simple event: delicious and nutritious but not time-consuming. Although the most commonplace dinner in my house is an entrée (some sort of protein) and a salad, sometimes when I am really craving vegetables, I do a tiny bit more work and make something uncomplicated—which for me is usually adding a bit of flavor to something fresh. Whether it's sautéing cherry or grape tomatoes in garlic and olive oil (page 91), or roasting broccoli with garlic and ginger (page 94), it has to be quick, easy and wonderful.

Grape Tomatoes with Garlic and Olive Oil

A simple, versatile last-minute side dish for steak, fish and chicken, this can also be used as a topping for burgers, as a sauce for pasta (just add Parmesan or feta cheese) or as a filling for an omelet with cheese and fresh herbs.

> "A world without tomatoes is like a string quartet without violins."
> —LAURIE COLWIN, WRITER (1944–1992)

SERVES 4

1 tablespoon olive oil

2 garlic cloves, pressed or finely chopped

2 pounds grape or cherry tomatoes

2 teaspoons chopped fresh rosemary, basil or oregano leaves,
    or 1 teaspoon dried rosemary, basil or oregano

Kosher salt and black pepper to taste

Place a large skillet over medium heat and when it is hot, add the oil. Add the garlic, tomatoes and rosemary and cook, covered, until tender, 12–15 minutes. Add salt and pepper to taste. Serve immediately, or cover and refrigerate up to overnight. Reheat before serving.

Maple Syrup–Glazed Baby Carrots

This dish has the colors and flavors of fall. Add a sprinkle of feta cheese and crushed red pepper flakes for a completely different effect.

> "I never worry about diets. The only carrots that interest me are the number you get in a diamond."
>
> —MAE WEST, ACTRESS (1893–1980)

SERVES 4–6

2 pounds baby carrots, or big carrots cut in baby-size chunks

1½ cups water

3 tablespoons unsalted butter

2 tablespoons maple syrup or brown sugar

2 teaspoons freshly grated lemon zest (optional)

2 tablespoons chopped fresh Italian flat-leaf parsley, dill or cilantro leaves

½–1 teaspoon kosher salt

½ teaspoon black pepper

Place the carrots and water in a medium-size pot and bring to a boil over high heat. Cover and boil for 3–4 minutes. Lower the heat to medium, add the butter and maple syrup, and cook until the water has been absorbed and the carrots are tender, 5–7 minutes.

Add the lemon zest, if desired, and the parsley, salt and pepper. Stir well and serve immediately.

Spinach with Garlic and Pine Nuts

This dish works well with either fish or chicken. Make more than you think you'll need; it's also good atop pasta or stuffed into an omelet.

Although SPINACH originated in the Middle East, it was often referred to as the Spanish vegetable because it was the Spaniards who introduced it to the UK and U.S. It is high in iron, oxalic acid, beta-carotene and vitamins B and C.

> "A food is not necessarily essential just because your child hates it."
> —KATHERINE WHITEHORN, JOURNALIST (B. 1926)

SERVES 4

1½–2 pounds fresh spinach, ends trimmed and discarded
2 teaspoons olive oil
2–4 garlic cloves, chopped
1–2 tablespoons pine nuts
¼ cup feta cheese, crumbled (optional)
Kosher salt and black pepper

Wash the spinach well and shake out the water. Place a large saucepan over high heat and add the spinach. Cook, stirring occasionally, until tender, 5–7 minutes. Transfer the spinach to a colander and set aside.

Place the saucepan over medium heat and when it is hot, add the oil. Add the garlic and pine nuts and cook until golden, 3–5 minutes. Return the spinach to the saucepan, toss to combine and cook until heated through, about 2 minutes. Add the feta cheese, if using, and salt and pepper to taste. Serve immediately.

Roasted Broccoli with Garlic and Ginger

Even die-hard broccoli haters will be persuaded to try this spicy variation.

> "I do not like broccoli. And I haven't liked it since I was a little kid and my mother made me eat it. And I'm President of the United States and I'm not going to eat any more broccoli."
>
> —GEORGE H. W. BUSH, STATESMAN (B. 1924)

SERVES 4

2 heads broccoli, florets and stalks, thickly sliced, separated

2 tablespoons olive oil

1 tablespoon finely chopped garlic

1 teaspoon finely chopped fresh gingerroot

½ teaspoon kosher salt

¼–½ teaspoon crushed red pepper flakes (optional)

1 lemon, quartered

Preheat the oven to 450 degrees.

Place the broccoli stalks (not the florets) in a medium-size bowl and cover with boiling water. Let stand 5 minutes. Drain off the water and add the florets, olive oil, garlic, ginger, salt and red pepper flakes, if desired, to the bowl. Toss well and transfer to a baking sheet. Place in the oven and roast until the broccoli is crisp-tender, 12–15 minutes. Serve immediately, with the lemon wedges.

Pan-Roasted Asparagus

This is my favorite way to cook asparagus, and it can be served with almost anything. Leftovers can be used in salads and omelets.

For a little variety you can add 2 garlic cloves in the beginning and/or 1 tablespoon drained capers at the end.

Happily, cooking asparagus is not time-consuming. In fact, the Roman emperor Augustus coined the phrase *Velocius quam asparagi conquantur,* meaning to do something even faster than the time it takes to cook asparagus (which is really fast).

Peel the asparagus, if desired, and get rid of the woody ends by bending the spear by hand; the spot where it snaps is the perfect point.

ASPARAGUS, a member of the lily family, has been cultivated for over 2,000 years. An Arab love manual recommends that you boil and fry asparagus and then cover it in egg yolk. Eaten daily, it was said to keep one virile and alert all night.

SERVES 6

2–2½ pounds asparagus, woody stems removed
2 tablespoons water
1 tablespoon olive oil
Juice of 1 lemon (about ¼ cup)
Kosher salt and black pepper
Freshly grated Parmesan cheese (optional)

Place the asparagus, water and olive oil in a large skillet and cook over high heat until the water has cooked off and the asparagus begins to lightly brown, 5–7 minutes. Add the lemon juice and cook for 1 minute. Add salt and pepper to taste. Serve immediately, garnished with freshly grated Parmesan cheese, if desired.

Mashed Potatoes

Nothing says comfort food like mashed potatoes. Serve them with meat loaf or anything else. Form leftovers into patties and cook them like a burger, or mix them with shredded cheese and bake in a casserole for an easy version of scalloped potatoes.

> "My friend said to me, You know what I like? Mashed potatoes. I was like, Dude, you have to give me time to guess. If you're going to quiz me you have to insert a pause."
>
> —MITCH HEDBERG, COMEDIAN (1968–2005)

SERVES 6–8

3 pounds small red potatoes, peeled if desired, and quartered
½ cup heavy cream
¼ cup unsalted butter, at room temperature
2 tablespoons freshly grated Parmesan cheese (optional)
Kosher salt and black pepper to taste

Place the potatoes in a large pot, cover with cold water and bring to a boil over high heat. Lower the heat to medium and cook until tender, 10–12 minutes.

Drain the potatoes and place them in a medium-size mixing bowl. Mash with a fork or potato masher, gradually incorporating the remaining ingredients. Serve immediately.

Potato Gratin
(or, in Boston, Scalloped Potatoes)

I had owned a gratin pan (a shallow oval enamel pan) for about ten years before I ever used it. Somehow the pan just begged for a real gratin and this one was just what I dreamed of: creamy and rich with a crusty top. Finally, a gratin worth having a pan for.

> "Only two things in this world are too serious to be jested on: potatoes and matrimony." —IRISH SAYING

SERVES 6–8

½ cup heavy cream
¾ cup whole milk
1 teaspoon kosher salt
1 garlic clove, minced
1 teaspoon dried thyme
Pinch black pepper
Pinch ground nutmeg
1¾–2 pounds new potatoes, cut in ⅛-inch-thick slices
2 cups shredded cheddar or Gruyère cheese (optional)
¼ cup freshly grated Parmesan cheese

Preheat the oven to 350 degrees. Lightly butter a gratin dish or an 8 x 8-inch baking pan.

Place the cream, milk, salt, garlic, thyme, pepper and nutmeg in a small saucepan and bring to a low boil. Lower the heat to low and cook until slightly thickened, 3–5 minutes. Place one-third of the potatoes in the buttered dish, add one-half of the cheddar and repeat until the potatoes are all added. Pour the hot cream over them. Press down with the back of a spoon.

Transfer to the oven and bake until the potatoes are tender, 45–55 minutes. Raise the oven temperature to 450 degrees, press the potatoes down again and sprinkle with the Parmesan. Continue baking until golden brown, about 15 minutes. Serve immediately.

Roasted Potatoes

This classic steakhouse side is a healthy alternative to French fries and a great breakfast accompaniment (without the garlic if you choose). You can substitute 1½ to 2 pounds sweet potatoes or yams for the new potatoes, or better yet, cook half of each.

NEW POTATOES are harvested in early summer when they are small and not fully matured and as a result have a sweet and mild flavor. Their tender, waxy white flesh and thin yellow or red skin make them perfect for boiling and turning into potato salad. In general eight to ten new potatoes equal one pound. When purchasing potatoes, be sure to avoid ones that have punctures on their surface or any soft spots. New potatoes should be used within four days of purchase and should be stored in a cool, dry place.

> "People have been cooking and eating for thousands of years, so if you are the very first to have thought of adding fresh lime juice to scalloped potatoes try to understand that there must be a reason for this."
>
> —FRAN LEBOWITZ, JOURNALIST (B. 1951)

SERVES 6–8

3 pounds new potatoes, halved or quartered
2 tablespoons olive oil
4–6 garlic cloves, finely chopped
1½ teaspoons kosher salt
2 teaspoons finely chopped fresh rosemary leaves

Preheat the oven to 450 degrees.

Place the potatoes in a large bowl. Add the olive oil, garlic and salt and mix until combined.

Place the mixture on a baking sheet or in a large baking pan and cook, stirring after 15 minutes, until browned, 35–45 minutes. Serve immediately, sprinkled with the rosemary.

Spicy Roasted Potatoes with Cilantro and Peppers

Strong flavors make this new twist on roasted potatoes more flavorful, if not quite as versatile—and frankly, hard to stop eating. It's good with simpler dishes like burgers, grilled steak and chicken. Try it with eggs instead of hash browns or home fries.

> "I have made a lot of mistakes falling in love, and regretted most of them, but never the potatoes that went with them."
>
> —NORA EPHRON, AUTHOR AND FILMMAKER (B. 1941)

SERVES 6–8

2 tablespoons canola or olive oil

1 tablespoon toasted sesame oil

2 tablespoons curry powder

4 garlic cloves, minced

2 teaspoons kosher salt

2 tablespoons dry sherry

3 pounds potatoes (about 24 small), halved or quartered

1 red bell pepper, diced

⅓–½ red onion, diced

½ cup chopped fresh cilantro leaves, for garnish

Preheat the oven to 450 degrees.

Place the oils, curry powder, garlic, salt and sherry in a small bowl and mix well. (This can be done a day ahead.)

Place the potatoes, bell pepper, onion and curry mixture in a large bowl and toss well. (This can be done 8 hours ahead.)

Transfer to a baking sheet, place in the oven and cook until golden brown, 45–50 minutes. Serve immediately, garnished with the cilantro.

Portobello Mushroom Pizza

This isn't really a side dish but rather a light summer supper or a lunch. My daughter, Lauren, loves these; she often takes them to school and reheats them in the microwave. These "pizzas" can be endlessly varied by adding cooked vegetables, pepperoni, Roasted Garlic (page 9), Caramelized Onions (page 10), or basically whatever you'd like on a pizza. Serve with a tossed salad.

> "It's bizarre that the produce manager is more important to my children's health than the pediatrician."
>
> —MERYL STREEP, ACTRESS (B. 1949)

SERVES 4

4 portobello mushroom caps, wiped clean
¼ cup pesto, homemade or store-bought
½ cup ricotta cheese
½ cup tomato sauce, homemade or store-bought
½ cup shredded mozzarella cheese
Dried oregano or chopped fresh oregano leaves to taste
Black pepper to taste

Preheat the oven to 400 degrees.

Place the caps, right side up, on a baking sheet. Transfer to the oven and bake until well roasted, about 25 minutes. Drain off any liquid.

Place the mushrooms stemmed side up on the baking sheet and top with 1 tablespoon pesto. Top each with 2 tablespoons ricotta and 2 tablespoons tomato sauce, and sprinkle with the mozzarella, oregano and black pepper. Return to the oven until the mozzarella has melted, about 3 minutes. Serve immediately.

Pasta and Rice

Like everyone else I know who has children, I cook an incalculable amount of pasta, especially for my son, Ben. My daughter, Lauren, loves pasta but prefers rice. Although they both eat real food, it would take a long time before they complained of eating only carbs. Fortunately they both are happy to have me experiment, and it's great to have a lot of effortless options.

No-Nonsense Ten-Minute Pasta Sauce

This sauce is the perfect one to make when there seems to be nothing in the house.

> "Do what you can, with what you have, where you are."
> —THEODORE ROOSEVELT, PRESIDENT OF THE UNITED STATES (1858–1919)

1 teaspoon olive oil
1 small Spanish onion, halved and chopped
4–6 garlic cloves, coarsely chopped
Five 16-ounce cans diced tomatoes, undrained
½ cup dry white or red wine
1 tablespoon dried basil
8 fresh basil leaves, chopped or julienned (optional)
Freshly grated Parmesan cheese (optional)

Place a large skillet over medium heat and when it is hot, add the olive oil. Add the onion and garlic and cook until tender, 5–7 minutes. Add the tomatoes, wine and dried basil. Cook until slightly thickened, about 10 minutes.

Serve over the pasta of your choice, garnished with the fresh basil and Parmesan cheese, if desired. Or cover and refrigerate up to 3 days or freeze up to 1 month.

Pasta with Garlic and Olive Oil

At Italian restaurants they call this pasta *aglio e olio*, but no matter the name, it's a quick and easy dish, great for a late-night supper when there's really nothing in the pantry. If you're lucky enough to have a loaf of bread or the ingredients for a Caesar salad (page 71), you have yourself a fine meal.

This sauce is most often served with spaghetti or linguini. You can add crushed red pepper flakes, fresh hot peppers, crumbled bacon or prosciutto, grated lemon zest, toasted pine nuts and/or chopped fresh basil leaves, depending on your mood, your taste, and what you have lying around.

> "Stop and smell the garlic! That's all you have to do."
> —WILLIAM SHATNER, ACTOR (B. 1931)

SERVES 4–6

1 pound spaghetti
¼ cup olive oil
6 garlic cloves, thinly sliced or coarsely chopped
Kosher salt and black pepper
Freshly grated Parmesan cheese, for garnish

Bring a large pot of water to a boil over high heat. Add the spaghetti and cook until al dente.

While the spaghetti is cooking, place a large skillet over medium-low heat and when it is hot, add the olive oil. Add the garlic and cook until golden, about 3 minutes.

Drain the spaghetti and add it to the skillet. Add salt and pepper to taste. Mix well and serve immediately, garnished with Parmesan cheese.

Pasta with Artichoke Hearts

I hate to admit (but must) that adding marinated artichokes to hot pasta sounds bizarre but is, in reality, truly delightful. This dish can be made more substantial by adding poached or grilled chicken, diced tomatoes and/or fresh mozzarella cubes.

Typically the heart is considered the tastiest and best part of an artichoke. Unfortunately it requires meticulous care to prepare it so as not to accidentally leave some of the "choke" attached. For a small price you can purchase marinated artichoke hearts that have been prepared, cooked and soaked in olive oil, vinegar, garlic, salt and black pepper. They are sold in either cans or jars and some may contain a hint of spice (such as crushed red pepper flakes).

> "After all the trouble you go to, you get about as much actual 'food' out of eating an artichoke as you would from licking 30 or 40 postage stamps."
> —"MISS PIGGY"

SERVES 4–6

1 pound medium-size shaped pasta, such as penne
2 tablespoons olive oil
1 large Spanish onion, halved and chopped
2 garlic cloves, minced
2 cups marinated artichoke hearts
½ teaspoon kosher salt
½ teaspoon black pepper
¼ cup chopped fresh basil leaves
¼ teaspoon crushed red pepper flakes (optional)
Freshly grated Parmesan cheese, for garnish

Bring a large pot of water to a boil over high heat. Add the pasta and cook until al dente.

While the pasta is cooking, place a large skillet over medium-low heat and when it is hot, add the olive oil. Add the onion and garlic and cook until soft, 5–7 minutes.

Add the artichokes and mash with a fork. Cook until heated through, about 2 minutes. Add the salt, pepper and basil. (The sauce can be made, covered and refrigerated up to 3 days ahead.)

Drain the pasta and add it to the skillet. Reserve a little bit of the pasta water in case you need to thin the sauce. Mix well and serve immediately with the crushed red pepper flakes, if desired, and the Parmesan cheese.

Pasta with Smoked Salmon

Smoked salmon doesn't last very long in my house, but on those rare occasions when there is some left over from a Sunday brunch, this pasta salad offers a perfect vehicle to use it up.

> "Spaghetti can be eaten most successfully if you inhale it like a vacuum cleaner."
>
> —SOPHIA LOREN, ACTRESS (B. 1934)

SERVES 6–8

For the dressing:

2 garlic cloves, chopped

1 tablespoon Dijon mustard

¼ cup fresh lemon or lime juice

¼ cup red wine vinegar

6 tablespoons olive oil

¼–⅓ cup chopped fresh cilantro leaves

For the pasta:

1–1½ pounds penne or other medium-size shaped pasta

½ pound smoked salmon, cut in strips

1 small red onion, halved and cut in thin strips

1 red bell pepper, cut in strips

3 tablespoons capers, drained and rinsed

¼ teaspoon kosher salt

¼ teaspoon black pepper

4 cups mesclun greens

TO MAKE THE DRESSING: Place the garlic, mustard, lemon juice and vinegar in a blender or a food processor fitted with a steel blade and blend until smooth. Gradually add the olive oil and blend until emulsified. Add the cilantro and pulse to combine. (The dressing can be made up to 3 days in advance.)

TO MAKE THE PASTA: Bring a large pot of water to a boil over high heat. Add the pasta and cook until al dente. Rinse well with cold water until it is cooled.

Transfer the pasta to a large bowl and toss with the dressing. Add the salmon, red onion, bell pepper, capers, salt and pepper and toss well. Divide the mesclun among four plates, top with equal amounts of the salad and serve immediately.

Pasta with Creamy Tomato Sauce

I've been making this creamy, chunky pasta sauce since I was in college, and while I have endlessly altered it, it never diverges too far from the original.

If you end up with a small amount of LEFTOVER WINE **and don't think you'll be using it soon, you can freeze it in ice cube trays for use in other recipes.**

> "I cook with wine, sometimes I even add it to the food."
> —W. C. FIELDS, COMEDIAN AND ACTOR (1880–1946)

SERVES 4–6

For the sauce:

1 tablespoon unsalted butter

1 red onion, halved and finely chopped

2 garlic cloves, chopped

3 carrots, diced

2 zucchini, diced

1 red bell pepper, diced

1 tablespoon dried basil

2 tablespoons chopped fresh Italian flat-leaf parsley leaves

One 28-ounce can diced tomatoes, undrained

½ cup dry white wine

1 teaspoon kosher salt

½ teaspoon black pepper

1 cup heavy or sour cream

2 tablespoons tomato paste

1 pound medium-size shaped pasta, such as shells or rotini

Freshly shaved or grated Parmesan cheese

Fresh basil leaves, for garnish

TO MAKE THE SAUCE: Place a large skillet over medium-high heat and when it is hot, add the butter. When the butter has melted, add the onion, garlic, carrots, zucchini, bell pepper, basil and parsley and cook until tender, 10–15 minutes.

Add the tomatoes, wine, salt and pepper and cook until all the vegetables are soft, 15–20 minutes.

Place the cream and tomato paste in a small bowl and stir to combine. Gradually add the mixture to the skillet and cook until heated through, 2–3 minutes, stirring all the while. (The sauce can be covered and refrigerated up to 3 days or frozen up to 3 weeks.)

Bring a large pot of water to a boil over high heat. Add the pasta and cook until al dente. Drain well and divide among shallow bowls. Reserve a little bit of the pasta water in case you need to thin the sauce.

Serve the pasta immediately, topped with the sauce and garnished with Parmesan cheese and basil.

Fettuccine Alfredo

Creamy and rich, this is the pasta my children beg for. In fact, my daughter, Lauren, swears she could eat it every day. And yet there's nothing childlike about it.

During the 1920s, Alfredo di Lelio created Fettuccine Alfredo at his restaurant in Rome, Alfredo all'Augusteo. Unlike many dishes that were created in the last century, Fettuccine Alfredo remains essentially the same: a combination of butter, heavy cream, freshly ground black pepper and Parmesan cheese.

Diverging from Alfredo's original recipe, I often add lightly steamed broccoli rabe at the end; it cuts the richness and makes this more of an everyday dish.

SERVES 4

I pound fettuccine or spaghetti
I tablespoon unsalted butter
I cup heavy cream
¼ cup Chicken Stock (page 8) or vegetable stock
¾ teaspoon kosher salt
¼–½ teaspoon black pepper
¾ cup freshly grated Parmesan cheese, plus more for garnish

Bring a large pot of water to a boil over high heat. Add the pasta and cook until al dente.

While the pasta is cooking, place the butter, cream and stock in a small saucepan and bring to a boil over medium-high heat. Lower the heat to medium and cook, stirring occasionally, until the mixture has reduced by half, about 5 minutes.

Add the salt, pepper and Parmesan cheese to the sauce, and stir until well blended.

Drain the pasta and place it in a large serving bowl. Reserve a little bit of the pasta water in case you need to thin the sauce. Add the sauce to the spaghetti and divide it among four shallow bowls. Serve immediately, garnished with additional Parmesan cheese.

Spaghetti Carbonara

In my house this is often referred to as "Bacon and Egg Noodles." It is another quick dish beloved by my children and their friends: it has the requisite and perfect combination of salty and creamy flavors.

You can substitute prosciutto or ham for the bacon, and add fresh or frozen green peas. Serve the pasta with a salad and a loaf of bread.

> "Life expectancy would grow by leaps and bounds if green vegetables smelled as good as bacon."
>
> —DOUG LARSON, AUTHOR

SERVES 4

1 pound spaghetti or linguini
½–1 pound bacon, chopped, or 2 ounces prosciutto or pancetta, chopped
½ cup dry white wine
1 cup finely grated Parmesan cheese
2 large eggs
2 large egg yolks
2 tablespoons finely chopped fresh Italian flat-leaf parsley leaves

Bring a large pot of water to a boil over high heat. Add the pasta and cook until al dente.

While the pasta is cooking, place the bacon in a large skillet over medium heat and cook until it is browned and rendered of fat, about 10 minutes. Pour off all but 2 tablespoons fat. Add the wine and bring to a boil. Set aside. (This can be done up to 8 hours ahead.)

Place the cheese, eggs and egg yolks in a large serving bowl and mix until smooth.

Using tongs, gradually transfer the pasta from the cooking pot to the egg mixture. (The pasta should be quite wet, but even so, reserve a little bit of the pasta water in case you need to thin the sauce.) While you are adding the pasta, mix it with the egg mixture. Continue adding pasta and mixing it until you have used it all. At the very end, it may be necessary to use a colander to drain off the remaining water. Add the bacon mixture and the parsley, and serve immediately.

Linguini with Shrimp and Feta Cheese

This dish tastes wonderful at room temperature, which means you can make it ahead of time if you're expecting dinner guests. Prepare the sauce early in the day and then cook the pasta later. Dinner can be on the table in ten minutes.

You can serve the sauce without the linguini; just have some good crusty bread on hand to sop up the juices.

The fabulous combination of salty and tangy flavor makes FETA, a classic Greek white cheese, one of my most beloved cheeses. Traditionally made from sheep or goat's milk, it is now typically made with pasteurized cow's milk, which is then salted and cured in brine. It is a great addition to salads and omelets.

SERVES 6

1 pound linguini
¼ cup olive oil
2–3 garlic cloves, minced
½ cup chopped fresh basil leaves
1 bunch scallions, chopped
¾ cup crumbled feta cheese
2 cups grape tomatoes
1 pound medium to large cooked shrimp
1 teaspoon kosher salt
½ teaspoon black pepper
Crushed red pepper flakes (optional)

Bring a large pot of water to a boil over high heat. Add the pasta and cook until al dente.

While the pasta is cooking, place the olive oil, garlic, basil, scallions, feta, tomatoes and shrimp in a large bowl and toss well. (The sauce can be made, covered and refrigerated up to 24 hours in advance.)

Add the pasta to the shrimp mixture and toss well. Add the salt, pepper and, if desired, red pepper flakes to taste. Serve immediately.

Spaghetti and Meatballs

The secret to forming meatballs is to keep your hands wet, which prevents the meat from sticking to your fingers. These meatballs, along with Provolone cheese and your favorite sandwich trimmings, can also be stuffed inside a baguette or a sub roll.

SERVES 6–8

For the tomato sauce:

1 tablespoon olive oil

½ Spanish onion, finely chopped

3 garlic cloves, finely chopped or crushed

2 tablespoons dried basil

1 tablespoon dried oregano

½ teaspoon crushed red pepper flakes

Two 28-ounce cans whole tomatoes, undrained

2 tablespoons tomato paste

½ cup dry red wine

Pinch sugar

For the meatballs:

1 slice white bread, torn in pieces

¼ cup whole milk

1–1¼ pounds ground beef or ground turkey

¼ cup finely chopped fresh Italian flat-leaf parsley leaves

1 large egg, beaten

2 tablespoons onion, finely chopped, or 3 scallions, coarsely chopped

1 teaspoon dried basil

1 teaspoon dried oregano

½ teaspoon black pepper

2–3 tablespoons freshly grated Parmesan cheese

1 tablespoon olive oil

1 pound spaghetti or linguini

TO MAKE THE TOMATO SAUCE: Place a large heavy-bottomed stockpot over medium heat and when it is hot, add the oil. Add the onion and garlic and cook until soft, 5–7 minutes. Add the remaining ingredients, and cook, partially covered, until thickened, 1½–2 hours. Stir occasionally. (The sauce can be refrigerated up to 2 days or frozen up to 2 months.)

TO MAKE THE MEATBALLS: Place the bread and milk in a large bowl and let sit until all the milk has been absorbed, about 5 minutes. Mash the mixture. Then add the beef, parsley, egg, onion, basil, oregano, pepper and Parmesan cheese and combine well. Divide into 24 parts and form into balls. (The meatballs can be covered and refrigerated up to 24 hours or frozen up to 2 months.)

Place a large skillet over medium heat and when it is hot, add the oil. Add the meatballs and cook until browned on all sides, about 5 minutes in all. Cover with the tomato sauce, lower the heat to low and cook until cooked through, about 15 minutes.

Bring a large pot of water to a boil over high heat. Add the pasta and cook until al dente. Serve with the meatballs and tomato sauce.

Classic Lasagna

It doesn't matter how many times I make lasagna: In spite of the fact that I always use the same ingredients, I never make it the same way twice. Sometimes I have just barely enough tomato sauce and sometimes I have lots left over. Sometimes the lasagna noodles curl; sometimes they lie flat. You just have to realize it's a rustic dish and not worry whether it will turn out picture-perfect.

If you want to freeze one or both lasagnas, line the pan with enough aluminum foil to hang over both sides. When the lasagna has set and/or cooked and cooled, you can lift it out of the pan by pulling up on the foil and placing the whole thing in a resealable plastic bag. This way you can freeze it without losing the use of the pan. You can also cut it and freeze it in individual pieces.

Although mozzarella is the general cheese of choice for lasagna, I prefer using Italian FONTINA. Primarily made from cow's milk, Fontina is a semi-firm pale yellow cheese that is mild, nutty and fruity all at once. It contains a high percentage of butterfat and therefore melts easily and uniformly to create a smooth texture; it is commonly used in fondue. Fontina is also manufactured in Sweden, America and Holland, but those varieties are bland compared to the Italian Fontina. Do not purchase Fontina that has visible cracks on the surface.

MAKES 2 LASAGNAS; EACH SERVES 6–8

Two 1-pound boxes lasagna noodles
2 pounds whole- or skim-milk ricotta cheese
4 large eggs
2 cups freshly grated Parmesan cheese
1 recipe Traditional Meat Sauce (page 186)
1½–2 pounds Fontina cheese or 2 pounds mozzarella,
    thinly sliced or grated

Bring a large pot of water to a boil over high heat. Add the pasta and cook until it is just barely al dente (the innermost center should be slightly dark and look slightly raw). Drain the pasta in a colander and rinse with cold water. Put the noodles back in the pot and add cold water to cover (the noodles are easier to use if wet).

Place the ricotta, eggs and 1 cup Parmesan cheese in a medium-size mixing bowl and mix to combine.

TO ASSEMBLE THE LASAGNA: Place 1 cup Traditional Meat Sauce in each of two 9 x 13-inch baking pans. In each pan, place a layer of noodles (about 3 across) on top of the sauce and then add dollops of the ricotta mixture (about one sixth of the mixture) on top of the noodles. Do not worry that the dollops don't cover the sauce; leave them as dollops. Sprinkle about one sixth of the Fontina over the ricotta. Add about 2 cups of the meat sauce. Repeat the layers of noodles, ricotta and Fontina twice. Then add another layer of noodles, sauce and Fontina. Top each with ½ cup of the remaining Parmesan cheese.

Cover each pan with plastic wrap, and press down on the layers to compact them. Refrigerate at least overnight and up to 3 days. You can also cover the pans with aluminum foil and freeze up to 2 months.

TO COOK THE LASAGNA: Preheat the oven to 350 degrees.

Remove the plastic wrap and cover the pans with aluminum foil. Transfer to the oven and bake for 15 minutes. Remove the foil and continue baking until the sauce is bubbling and the top is lightly browned, 25–30 minutes. Set aside to cool for about 10 minutes. Serve immediately, or cover and refrigerate up to 3 days.

Baked Pasta with Mozzarella and Tomato

You could call this lazy man's lasagna, but it's really a cross between lasagna and Mac and Cheese. It's a perfect solution when you want the taste of lasagna but don't want to do all the work. Assemble it in the morning and bake it at night.

> "Life is a combination of magic and pasta."
> —FEDERICO FELLINI, FILMMAKER (1920–1993)

SERVES 6–8

4–5 cups Traditional Meat Sauce (page 186) or No-Nonsense Ten-Minute
    Pasta Sauce (page 102)
¾ pound medium-size shaped pasta, such as penne, cooked and cooled
1 pound fresh or American mozzarella cheese, cubed
½ cup finely grated Parmesan cheese

Preheat the oven to 400 degrees.

Place the sauce and pasta in a large bowl and mix well. Transfer about one third of this mixture to a 9 x 13-inch pan and top it with one third of the mozzarella cheese. Repeat the layers twice and then top with the Parmesan. (You can cover and refrigerate up to 2 days.)

Transfer the pan to the oven and bake until the sauce is bubbling and the top is lightly browned, 20–30 minutes. Set aside to cool for about 10 minutes. Serve immediately, or cover and refrigerate up to 3 days.

Macaroni and Cheese

Finally, a Mac and Cheese that kids will love and parents will be happy to serve.

If you want to freeze this, line the pan with enough aluminum foil to hang over both sides. When it has set and/or cooked and cooled, you can lift it out of the pan by pulling up on the foil and placing the whole thing in a resealable plastic bag. This way you can freeze it without losing the use of the pan. You can also cut it and freeze it in individual pieces.

> "Memories, imagination, old sentiments, and associations are more readily reached through the sense of smell than through any other channel."
> —OLIVER WENDELL HOLMES, WRITER (1809–1894)

SERVES 6–8

For the pasta:

1 pound shaped pasta, such as macaroni, cavatappi, shells or tubes
¼ cup unsalted butter
¼ cup all-purpose flour
½ teaspoon kosher salt
⅛–¼ teaspoon white pepper
2½ cups whole milk
2½–3 cups grated cheddar cheese
1 cup grated Gruyère cheese
1 cup freshly grated Parmesan cheese
¼ cup fresh basil leaves, chopped (optional)
One 28-ounce can whole tomatoes, well drained and chopped (optional)

For the topping:

½–⅓ cup Romano cheese
2 cups Bread Crumbs (page 11)

(Continued on next page)

Preheat the oven to 350 degrees.

TO MAKE THE PASTA: Bring a large pot of water to a boil over high heat. Add the pasta and cook until al dente. Drain and transfer to a large mixing bowl.

Place the butter in a large pan and cook over low heat until it melts. Gradually add the flour, salt and pepper, stirring all the time. As soon as it thickens, gradually add the milk, whisking constantly until the mixture has the consistency of heavy cream, about 1 minute. Gradually add the cheddar, Gruyère and Parmesan cheeses, stirring all the time. Add the cheese mixture to the pasta and stir to combine.

Stir in the basil and tomatoes, if desired, and place in a 9 x 13-inch baking dish.

TO MAKE THE TOPPING: Combine the Romano and bread crumbs in a small bowl, and sprinkle evenly over the pasta. (You can cover and refrigerate the dish up to 2 days or freeze up to 3 months.) Bake until golden brown, 35–40 minutes. Serve immediately.

Four-Cheese Pasta

Mac and Cheese for grown-ups.

ROMANO versus PARMESAN: While many recipes make no distinction between Parmesan and Romano cheese, they are in fact very different. Romano, not to be confused with Pecorino Romano (an aged Italian sheep's milk cheese), is an American-made cow's milk cheese. It is a hard, pale yellow cheese, perfect for grating over pasta, with a subtle but sharp flavor. Parmesan is a cow's milk cheese made in either America or Italy. Italian Parmesan, known as Parmigiano Reggiano, is preferable to the American variety. Like Romano, it is a hard cheese, perfect for grating over pasta. Fruity, nutty, sweet, and salty, Parmesan is aged at least 14 months and has a much stronger and more complicated flavor. Authentic Parmigiano Reggiano is marked with a stamp, showing the date it was made. While Romano and Parmesan are used in the same way, they are not interchangeable. Avoid cheese that is dried out or that has a white layer on its surface. While the rind is inedible, it adds a tremendous amount of flavor to soups. Both Romano and Parmesan should be stored in the refrigerator, wrapped in a moist towel and then in aluminum foil so that the cheese is able to breathe. If small bits of surface mold appear, don't discard the cheese; just scrape them off.

GORGONZOLA is an Italian blue-veined cheese made from cow's milk. There are two distinct types, *dolce* (sweet) and *naturale* (aged), each of which has a distinct flavor and odor. *Dolce* Gorgonzola, the most common variety, is a fragrant, soft, mild cheese. Its interior is ivory in color and its veins are a greenish blue. It is often served as part of a cheese plate, or crumbled and served in a salad. *Naturale* Gorgonzola has a stronger and more pungent flavor, which comes from having been aged for more than 1 year. It has a much thicker rind; its interior is whiter and its veins are bluer. In general, try to buy Gorgonzola in large chunks that are wrapped in either foil or plastic; this will ensure that it has retained the most flavor and butterfat. Avoid cheese that has a brown or gray interior, or that is leaking butterfat.

SERVES 6–8

For the bread crumb topping:

1½ cups Bread Crumbs (page 11)
¼ cup freshly grated Parmesan cheese
¼ teaspoon kosher salt
⅛ teaspoon black pepper

For the pasta:

1 pound medium-size shaped pasta, such as penne
1 cup shredded Italian Fontina cheese
¾ cup crumbled Gorgonzola cheese
½ cup grated Romano cheese
¼ cup freshly grated Parmesan cheese
¼ teaspoon kosher salt
¼ teaspoon black pepper
2 teaspoons unsalted butter
2 teaspoons all-purpose flour
1½ cups heavy cream

(Continued on next page)

Preheat the oven to 500 degrees.

TO PREPARE THE TOPPING: Place the bread crumbs, Parmesan cheese, salt and pepper in a small bowl, mix to combine and set aside.

TO PREPARE THE PASTA: Bring a large pot of water to a boil over high heat. Add the pasta and cook until it is just barely al dente (the innermost center is still dark and looks slightly raw). Transfer the pasta to a colander and drain for about 5 seconds, leaving it slightly wet.

Place the Fontina, Gorgonzola, Romano and Parmesan cheeses, along with the salt and pepper, in a large mixing bowl. Stir well and set aside.

Place the butter in a small saucepan and melt it over medium heat. Add the flour and whisk until smooth, about 30 seconds. Gradually add the cream and cook until it just comes to a boil. Add the pasta to the bowl of cheeses and then add the cream sauce. Cover the bowl with a plate and let sit for 3 minutes. Stir well, being careful to mix in the cheeses from the bottom, and transfer to a 9 x 13-inch glass, aluminum or ceramic pan. (You can cover and refrigerate the dish up to 2 days before cooking.)

Sprinkle the bread crumb topping over the pasta, pressing it down lightly. Transfer the pan to the oven and bake until the topping is golden brown, 6–7 minutes. Serve immediately.

> "I am not a glutton—I am an explorer of food."
> —ERMA BOMBECK, HUMORIST (1927–1996)

Variations

TOMATO-BASIL: When you add the cream, stir in one 16-ounce can diced tomatoes, drained. Just prior to transferring the pasta to the pan, stir in ¼ cup coarsely chopped fresh basil leaves.

PROSCIUTTO-PEA: Omit the salt from the cheese mixture. When you add the cream, add 4 ounces chopped prosciutto. Just prior to transferring the pasta to the pan, stir in 1 cup frozen peas.

Curried Rice–Stuffed Peppers

This is a wonderful side or luncheon dish. The rice can also stand alone. Ben, my twelve-year-old son, and Michael, my twenty-three year-old nephew, both love this dish.

SERVES 6

1 tablespoon olive oil
1 large Spanish onion, halved and chopped
1 garlic clove, minced
1 tablespoon curry powder
1 cup long-grain rice
2 cups water
6 red, orange, green or yellow bell peppers, or a combination
⅓ cup currants, raisins or dried cherries
⅓ cup lightly toasted sliced almonds, chopped walnuts or chopped pecans (page 12)
3–4 tablespoons chopped fresh dill leaves
3–4 tablespoons chopped fresh mint leaves

Preheat the oven to 450 degrees.

Place a medium-size saucepan over medium heat and when it is hot, add the olive oil. Add the onion, garlic and curry powder and cook until the onion is soft, 5–7 minutes. Add the rice and water, and bring to a boil. Cover and lower the heat to the lowest possible heat. Cook for 20 minutes.

Cut off and coarsely chop the tops of the peppers. Scoop out and discard the insides of the peppers. Place the peppers, except the tops, in a baking pan so that they are snug.

Remove the rice from the pan and place it in a mixing bowl. Add the chopped pepper tops, currants, nuts, dill and mint, and mix well. Divide the rice evenly among the peppers and place the pan in the oven. Cook until the peppers are soft, about 30 minutes. Serve immediately.

Sautéed Rice with Spinach and Feta Cheese

This is terrific with Roasted Chicken with Artichokes, Lemon and Onions (page 162), stuffed into bell peppers (as in the previous recipe) or as stuffing in a whole chicken (page 156).

For even more flavor, just prior to serving, add grated lemon zest, Kalamata olives, green olives, chopped scallions, chopped red onion or chopped prosciutto.

> "I don't like spinach, and I'm glad I don't, because if I liked it I'd eat it, and I just hate it."
>
> —CLARENCE DARROW, LAWYER (1857–1938)

SERVES 3–4

1 tablespoon unsalted butter

1 cup jasmine rice

2¼ cups water

1 cup chopped fresh flat-leaf spinach leaves

3–4 tablespoons crumbled feta cheese

½–1 teaspoon kosher salt

¼ teaspoon black pepper

Place a large skillet over medium-high heat and when it is hot, add the butter. When the butter has melted, add the rice and cook, stirring, until it begins to turn golden brown, about 7 minutes.

Add the water, ¼ cup at a time, and cook, waiting until it has been absorbed between additions, about 15 minutes. Add the remaining ingredients and cook, stirring all the while, until heated through, about 2 minutes. Serve immediately.

Poultry

"Poultry is for the cook what canvas is for the painter."

—JEAN-ANTHELME BRILLAT-SAVARIN, FRENCH GASTRONOME (1755–1826)

It's been said that poultry is like a little black dress: It is perfect as is, and when dressed up, it can be fabulous. It is equally at home at a Little League baseball game, a champagne reception for a visiting dignitary and a simple homemade dinner for two. It depends on what you do with it: accessorize with something unique and be elegant, or pair it with what's around and be casual. It's easy to cook, easy to improvise with and easy on the waistline. It can be eaten hot, cold or at room temperature; it can be brined, poached, fricasseed, stuffed, roasted, broiled, boiled, sautéed, grilled, microwaved, stewed and baked. It can be made either spicy or bland, eaten on the bone, off the bone, with skin, without skin, at home or on the run, between pieces of bread, in chilis, soups, omelets and savory pies, as a whole or in parts. It's good for people on high-protein diets, low-protein diets, fat-free diets, kosher diets and low-sodium diets, and for those on no diet at all. It can be eaten for breakfast, lunch and dinner and, barring dessert, at every course. In short, poultry is the perfect food.

Chicken Wings, Thighs and Drumettes

Sticky Orange Soy Trio

This recipe has saved the day when my children are being picky and nothing else appeals to them. As tasty cold as hot, this wonderful combination of sweet, salty and sticky satisfies them every time.

SERVES 6 GENEROUSLY

6 pounds chicken wings, tips removed, or drumettes, trimmed
1 cup soy sauce
½ cup frozen orange juice concentrate
½ cup light brown sugar
2–3 garlic cloves, minced
1 small chunk fresh gingerroot, minced
1–2 teaspoons crushed red pepper flakes (optional)

Place everything in a large glass, ceramic or plastic container, or in a resealable plastic bag, cover or seal, and refrigerate at least 4 hours and up to 2 days. (It can be frozen up to 2 months.)

Preheat the oven to 450 degrees.

Place the contents, including the marinade, in a large baking pan and transfer to the oven. Bake until the chicken is crispy and the marinade is sticky, 40–45 minutes. Serve immediately, or cover and refrigerate up to overnight.

Tabasco Trio

This spicy option for chicken wings or drumettes makes a delicious party hors d'oeuvre or an entrée for an informal dinner.

Although WORCESTERSHIRE SAUCE is a staple in most American households, few people actually know what it contains. Accurately described on its label as tangy and robust, Worcestershire sauce was first bottled in Worcestershire, England (although it originated in India). It is made from vinegar, molasses, anchovies, soy, onion, tamarind (a sweet-and-sour pulp taken from the fruit of a tree native to Asia) and other seasonings, and is most often found in Bloody Marys and in marinades for meat.

SERVES 6 GENEROUSLY

6 pounds chicken wings, wing tips removed, *or* bone-in, skin-on chicken thigh,
    or drumettes, trimmed of fat and patted dry
2 tablespoons garlic cloves
2 tablespoons Dijon mustard
1 tablespoon Worcestershire sauce
2 teaspoons Tabasco sauce
2 tablespoons olive oil
Juice of 1 lemon (about ¼ cup)

Place everything in a large glass, ceramic or plastic container or a resealable plastic bag, cover or seal, and refrigerate at least 4 hours and up to 2 days. (It can be frozen up to two months.)

Preheat the oven to 450 degrees.

Place the contents, including the marinade, in a large baking pan and transfer to the oven. Bake until the chicken is crispy, 40–45 minutes. Serve immediately, or cover and refrigerate up to overnight.

Boston Trio

Though I love New York's Buffalo Chicken Wings (deep-fried chicken wings doused in a spicy sauce), I am not fond of fried foods and decided to come up with a non-fried version. Like Buffalo Wings, these are great served with Blue Cheese Dressing (page 73) and also with Mango Salsa/Chutney (page 23).

> "I have just returned from Boston. It is the only thing to do if you find yourself up there."
>
> —FRED ALLEN, COMEDIAN (1894–1956)

SERVES 6 GENEROUSLY

¼ cup fresh lemon juice

¼ cup olive oil

2 tablespoons crushed red pepper flakes

1 tablespoon black pepper

1 tablespoon kosher salt

2 teaspoons dried thyme

6 pounds chicken wings, wing tips removed, *or* bone-in, skin-on chicken thighs, *or* drumettes, trimmed of fat and patted dry

Place the lemon juice, olive oil, red pepper flakes, black pepper, salt and thyme in a large glass, ceramic or plastic container or a resealable plastic bag. Mix well and add the chicken. Mix again, cover or seal, and refrigerate at least 4 hours and up to overnight. (It can be frozen up to 2 months.)

Preheat the broiler or prepare a grill.

Place the chicken on a rack in a broiler pan, or on the grill, and cook about 6 inches from the heat source until the skin is a deep, crispy brown and the fat has rendered, about 8 minutes on each side. Serve immediately.

Barbara and Bob's Chicken Thighs

I know a lot of people who make this every week. Serve it with a salad of Belgian endive, cherry tomatoes and fresh mozzarella balls; Caesar Salad (page 71) or greens drizzled with Blue Cheese Dressing (page 73).

SERVES 4

8 bone-in, skin-on chicken thighs, trimmed of fat and patted dry

4 garlic cloves, thickly sliced

1 tablespoon fresh rosemary leaves or 1 teaspoon dried rosemary (optional)

1½ tablespoons olive oil

Juice of 1 lemon

1 teaspoon kosher salt

½ teaspoon black pepper

Preheat the oven to 425 degrees.

Place the chicken in a single layer in a large roasting pan. Place the garlic slices and rosemary, if using, under the skin. Rub the olive oil and lemon juice over the chicken. (It can be frozen up to 2 months.)

Sprinkle with the salt and pepper. Transfer to the oven and bake until well browned and crispy, 1¼–1½ hours. Serve immediately, or cover and refrigerate up to overnight.

Crunchy Mustard Chicken

This baked "fried chicken" is equally good served hot or cold. Serve it hot with buttered rice or pasta and broccoli, asparagus or broccoli rabe, or cold with an assortment of salads.

> "I look upon it, that he who does not mind his belly will hardly mind anything else."
>
> —SAMUEL JOHNSON, LEXICOGRAPHER AND CRITIC (1709–1784)

SERVES 4

8 bone-in, skin-on chicken thighs, *or* 4 bone-in, skin-on chicken
    breast halves, trimmed of fat
2 tablespoons Dijon mustard
2 teaspoons light brown sugar
3 tablespoons Toasted Bread Crumbs (page 11)
1 teaspoon dried basil or tarragon
1 teaspoon kosher salt
½ teaspoon black pepper
1 lemon or lime, quartered

Preheat the oven to 500 degrees.

Place the chicken thighs in a baking dish, coat them with the mustard and then sprinkle with the brown sugar, bread crumbs, basil, salt and pepper.

Transfer to the oven and cook until they are well browned and cooked through, about 45 minutes for thighs and 20–25 minutes for breasts. If you want an extremely crunchy skin, broil for the last 2–3 minutes. Serve immediately with the lemon quarters, or cover and refrigerate at least 4 hours and up to 8 hours.

Braised Chicken Thighs
with Escarole

I never liked chicken thighs until I tasted this dish. Homey and flavorful, this braise is great for a weekday meal (which you can prep and freeze ahead) and truly spectacular for a dinner party. It's best to make this the day before you want to serve it, in order to let the flavors develop.

You can substitute kale or broccoli rabe for the escarole. Serve the chicken with mashed potatoes, polenta, rice and/or French bread.

In the same family as endive and thankfully available all year long, ESCAROLE is a very sturdy, slightly bitter green that can be added to salads but also stands up well to braising.

SERVES 6–8

4 sweet or spicy Italian sausages, pricked with a fork and cut in big chunks

8 bone-in, skin-on chicken thighs, trimmed of fat and patted dry

1 teaspoon kosher salt

½ teaspoon black pepper

½ red onion, chopped

8 garlic cloves, thinly sliced

1 teaspoon dried thyme

1 teaspoon dried rosemary

½ cup dry white wine

2 cups Chicken Stock (page 8)

½ cup green olives, pitted

1 large head escarole (about 1 pound), stem removed
    and leaves coarsely chopped

Place a large skillet over medium-high heat and when it is hot, add the sausages. Cook, turning occasionally, until they are browned, about 10 minutes. Transfer the sausages to a paper-towel-lined plate and set aside. Cover and refrigerate.

Remove all but 1 tablespoon fat from the skillet.

Sprinkle the chicken with the salt and pepper. Reheat the skillet and add the chicken, skin side down. Cook until well browned, about 4 minutes per side. Lower the heat to low and pour off all but 1 tablespoon fat. Add the onion, garlic, thyme and rosemary and cook for 10 minutes. Add the wine and chicken stock and continue cooking, turning the chicken halfway through, until the meat starts to fall away from the bone, about 1 hour. Using tongs, remove the chicken and set it aside with the sausage.

Add the green olives and escarole to the skillet and cook until the escarole wilts, about 10 minutes. Return the chicken and sausage to the pan and cook for 10 minutes.

Let the mixture cool, and then skim off and discard the fat. Cover and refrigerate overnight, or place in a resealable plastic bag and freeze for up to 2 months. If frozen, defrost. Reheat by placing over medium heat and cooking until warmed through, about 10 minutes.

Coq au Blanc

A white version of Coq au Vin, this is great winter fare, similar to Braised Chicken Thighs with Escarole (page 132) and also best made a day ahead. Serve it with a loaf of French bread to sop up the wonderful juices.

> "The golden rule when reading the menu is, if you cannot pronounce it, you cannot afford it."
>
> —FRANK MUIR, COMEDIAN (1920–1998)

SERVES 4

8 bone-in, skin-on chicken thighs, trimmed of fat and patted dry
1 teaspoon kosher salt
½ teaspoon black pepper
½ pound button mushrooms, sliced
2 carrots, chopped
1 celery stalk, chopped
1 Spanish onion, halved and chopped
3–4 garlic cloves, thinly sliced
1 teaspoon dried thyme
2 cups dry white wine
2 cups Chicken Stock (page 8)
¼ cup chopped fresh Italian flat-leaf parsley leaves

Sprinkle the chicken with the salt and pepper. Place a skillet over medium-high heat and when it is hot, add the thighs, skin side down, and sear until well browned, about 4 minutes per side. Using tongs, remove the chicken and set it aside on a plate.

Pour off all but a surface coating of the fat. Lower the heat to low, add the mushrooms, carrots, celery, onion, garlic and thyme, and cook until the vegetables are soft and golden, 10–15 minutes. Add the wine and chicken stock, return the chicken to the skillet and bring to a low boil. Cook, turning the chicken halfway through, until the meat falls away from bone, about 1 hour.

Let the mixture cool, and then skim off and discard the fat. Cover and refrigerate overnight, or place in a resealable plastic bag and freeze for up to 2 months. If frozen, defrost first. Reheat by placing over medium heat and cooking until warmed throughout, about 10 minutes. Sprinkle with the chopped parsley, and serve.

Skinless, Boneless Chicken Breasts

For maximum flavor distribution when cooking chicken breasts, flatten each breast by placing it between two pieces of waxed paper or plastic wrap and pounding it with a mallet, rolling pin or bottle until it is approximately ¼-inch thick.

Chicken with Balsamic Vinaigrette and Wilted Greens

Add a baguette to this summery dinner and *voilà*! You have your meal.

For a dish with Indian flavors, add 1 tablespoon curry powder to the marinade.

Leftover chicken can be added to a green salad or used in place of poached chicken in any of the chicken salads (pages 84–88).

SERVES 6–8

For the marinade:

3–4 garlic cloves

1 tablespoon Dijon mustard

¾ cup balsamic vinegar

¾ cup olive oil

1 teaspoon kosher salt

½ teaspoon black pepper

6–8 boneless, skinless chicken breast halves (about 3 pounds), trimmed of fat
   and membrane, pounded to an even thickness

1 teaspoon kosher salt

½ teaspoon black pepper

1 tablespoon olive oil

1 pound "Spring Mix" (assorted greens such as romaine, watercress, endive,
   radicchio, frisée) or "Mesclun Mix" (assorted baby greens)

TO PREPARE THE MARINADE: Place all the ingredients in a blender or a food processor fitted with a steel blade, and blend until the mixture starts to thicken. (The marinade can be made up to 1 week ahead.)

Place the chicken breasts in a large shallow ceramic or glass container, or in a re-sealable plastic bag, add half the marinade and mix well. (The chicken can be frozen at this point.) Cover and refrigerate for at least 4 hours and up to overnight. Transfer the remaining marinade to a bottle or glass jar, cover and refrigerate until ready to use.

Drain the chicken breasts, discarding the used marinade, and pat dry with a paper towel. Sprinkle the chicken with the salt and pepper.

Place a large nonstick or cast-iron skillet over high heat and when it is hot, add the olive oil. Add the chicken breasts, one at a time, allowing the pan to reheat for about 30 seconds between additions. Cook until the chicken is deeply browned and the juices run clear, 3–5 minutes per side, depending on the thickness. You will probably need to cook the chicken in two batches.

Serve the hot chicken breasts, whole or shredded, over the greens; the heat will wilt the greens. Drizzle with the reserved marinade. (If you don't like wilted greens, simply allow the chicken to cool before serving.)

Parmesan Chicken

Not to be confused with Chicken Parmesan, which is fairly heavy and smothered with tomato sauce, Parmesan Chicken is, while breaded, very light and almost delicate. If you leave out the pepper, this dish is a winner with most children, even the picky eaters.

Serve it with Caesar Salad (page 71) or Grape Tomatoes with Garlic and Olive Oil (page 91), steamed or roasted broccoli, or broccoli rabe.

These chicken breasts are also great served, hot or cold, in hollowed out baguettes with fresh mozzarella cheese and, if desired, sliced tomatoes.

For a no-fuss hot-weather meal, toss salad greens with Lemon Pepper Dressing (page 68). Place a mound of salad on a plate and top with a chicken breast. Serve with extra grated Parmesan.

SERVES 6–8

6–8 boneless, skinless chicken breast halves (about 3 pounds), trimmed of fat
    and membrane, pounded to an even thickness

¼ cup fresh lemon juice

2 teaspoons kosher salt

1½ teaspoons black pepper or crushed red pepper flakes (optional)

½ cup all-purpose flour

2 large eggs

¼ cup water

1 cup Toasted Bread Crumbs (page 11)

½ cup finely grated Parmesan cheese

1 tablespoon dried oregano

1 tablespoon dried basil

1 tablespoon olive oil

1 tablespoon unsalted butter

Place the chicken and the lemon juice in a large ceramic or glass mixing bowl, or in a resealable plastic bag, cover or seal, and refrigerate for at least 30 minutes but no more than 1 hour. Drain the chicken breasts, discarding the lemon juice. Pat dry with a paper towel. This is a very important step; if the chicken is not dry, the coating will not stick.

Sprinkle the chicken with the salt and pepper. Place the flour on a large plate. Place the eggs and water in a shallow bowl and whisk until uniform. Place the bread crumbs, Parmesan, oregano and basil on another large plate and mix to combine.

Dredge the chicken in the flour, shaking off any excess, and then in the eggs, again removing any excess. Dip in the bread crumb mixture to coat.

Place the breaded chicken on a wire rack, if you have one. If not, place it on a plate covered with waxed paper. Refrigerate, uncovered, at least ½ hour and up to 4 hours.

Preheat the oven to 200 degrees.

Place a large nonstick or cast-iron skillet over high heat. When the skillet is hot, add the olive oil and butter. When the butter has melted, add the chicken breasts one at a time, allowing the pan to reheat for about 30 seconds between additions. Cook until the chicken is deeply browned and the juices run clear, 3–5 minutes per side, depending on the thickness. You will probably need to cook the chicken in two batches.

As they are cooked, transfer the chicken breasts to a sheet pan and keep them warm in the oven for up to 15 minutes.

Chicken with Lemon and Ginger

Light and a little bit spicy. Serve this with Pasta with Artichoke Hearts (page 104), or with steamed rice and roasted broccoli.

> "If it weren't for Philo T. Farnsworth, inventor of television, we'd still be eating frozen radio dinners."
>
> —JOHNNY CARSON, TALK SHOW HOST AND COMEDIAN (1925–2005)

SERVES 6–8

2 tablespoons minced fresh gingerroot

3–4 garlic cloves, minced

Grated zest of 1 lemon

1 teaspoon crushed red pepper flakes

6–8 boneless, skinless chicken breast halves (about 3 pounds), trimmed of fat and membrane, pounded to an even thickness

1½ teaspoons kosher salt

½ teaspoon black pepper

1 tablespoon olive oil

2 lemons, quartered

Place the ginger, garlic, lemon zest and red pepper flakes in a medium-size glass or ceramic bowl, or in a resealable plastic bag, and mix well. Add the chicken and mix again. Cover or seal, and refrigerate at least 30 minutes but no longer than 2 hours. (If you want to freeze this, do it immediately; do not let it marinate at all.)

Drain the chicken, discarding the marinade. Pat it dry with a paper towel and sprinkle with the salt and pepper.

Place a large nonstick or cast-iron skillet over high heat and when it is hot, add the olive oil. Add the chicken breasts, one at a time, allowing the pan to reheat for about 30 seconds between additions. Cook until deeply browned and the juices run clear, 3–5 minutes per side. You will probably need to cook the chicken in two batches.

Transfer the chicken to a platter and serve immediately, garnished with the lemon quarters.

My Father's Lemon Tarragon Chicken

This is the only dish my father ever made while I was growing up. He also made this with shrimp, which was equally scrumptious.

> "Nothing revives the past so completely as a smell that was once associated with it."
>
> —VLADIMIR NABOKOV, NOVELIST (1899–1977)

SERVES 6–8

6–8 boneless, skinless chicken breast halves (about 3 pounds), trimmed of fat and membrane, pounded to an even thickness
¼ cup fresh lemon juice
2 teaspoons kosher salt
½ teaspoon black pepper
½ cup all-purpose flour
2 large eggs
2 tablespoons cold water
1 cup Toasted Bread Crumbs (page 11)
1 tablespoon dried tarragon
2 teaspoons dried basil
1 tablespoon olive oil
1 tablespoon unsalted butter
2 lemons, quartered

Place the chicken and the lemon juice in a large ceramic or glass mixing bowl or in a resealable plastic bag. Cover or seal, and refrigerate at least 30 minutes but no more than 1 hour. Drain the chicken breasts, discarding the lemon juice. Pat dry with a paper towel. This is a very important step; if the chicken is not dry, the coating will not stick.

(Continued on next page)

Sprinkle the chicken with the salt and pepper. Place the flour on a large plate. Place the eggs and water in a shallow bowl and whisk until uniform. Place the bread crumbs, tarragon and basil on another large plate and mix well.

Dredge the chicken in the flour, shaking off any excess, and then in the eggs, again removing any excess. Dip in the bread crumb mixture to coat.

Place the breaded chicken on a wire rack, if you have one. If not, place it on a plate covered with waxed paper. Refrigerate at least ½ hour and up to 4 hours. Do not cover it; you want it to air-dry.

Preheat the oven to 200 degrees.

Place a large nonstick or cast-iron skillet over medium-high heat. When the skillet is hot, add the olive oil and butter. When the butter has melted, add the chicken breasts one at a time, allowing the pan to reheat for about 30 seconds between additions. Cook until the chicken is deeply browned and the juices run clear, 3–5 minutes per side, depending on the thickness. You will probably need to cook the chicken in two batches.

As they are cooked, transfer the chicken breasts to a sheet pan and keep them warm in the oven for up to 15 minutes.

Serve garnished with the lemon quarters.

Tandoori Chicken

The buttermilk marinade transforms these chicken breasts into a deeply flavorful (but not spicy) meal. Serve it with roasted potatoes or rice, or save the starch for dessert and serve Rice Pudding (page 288).

TANDOORI refers to food has been cooked in a TANDOOR, the clay and brick oven used in India to cook meats and spices over very high heat. More recently, it has come to refer to the *kind* of foods usually prepared in one—whether they actually are or not.

Most commonly used in Asian cooking, TURMERIC, the spice that gives curry powder its gorgeous yellow orange hue, is aromatic and spicy.

SERVES 6–8

For the marinade:

¾ cup buttermilk or yogurt

¼ cup olive oil

Juice and grated zest of 1 lime

4–6 garlic cloves, minced

1 heaping tablespoon finely chopped fresh gingerroot

1 teaspoon chili powder

1 teaspoon turmeric

½ teaspoon ground cumin

6–8 boneless, skinless chicken breast halves (about 3 pounds), trimmed of fat
and membrane, pounded to an even thickness

1½ teaspoons kosher salt

½–1 teaspoon black pepper

1–2 tablespoons olive oil

TO PREPARE THE MARINADE: Place the buttermilk, olive oil, lime juice and zest, garlic, ginger, chili powder, turmeric and cumin in a large bowl, or in a resealable plastic bag, and mix well. Add the chicken breasts and mix again. Cover or seal, and refrigerate at least 4 hours and up to overnight. (You can freeze it at this point.)

Take the chicken out of the marinade and drain it, discarding the marinade. Pat dry with a paper towel and sprinkle with the salt and pepper.

Place a large nonstick or cast-iron skillet over high heat and when it is hot, add the oil. Add the chicken breasts one at a time, allowing the pan to reheat for about 30 seconds between additions. Cook until the chicken is deeply browned and the juices run clear, 3–5 minutes per side, depending on the thickness. You will probably need to cook the chicken in two batches.

Serve immediately.

Moroccan Chicken

This subtly spiced chicken is superb served atop couscous flavored with sliced almonds, chopped mint and cilantro.

> "Some people like to paint pictures, or do gardening, or build a boat in the basement. Other people get a tremendous pleasure out of the kitchen, because cooking is just as creative and imaginative an activity as drawing, or wood carving, or music."
> —JULIA CHILD, CHEF AND COOKBOOK AUTHOR (1912–2004)

SERVES 6–8

For the marinade:

¼ cup olive oil

2–3 garlic cloves, minced

2 teaspoons ground cumin

1 teaspoon ground ginger

1 teaspoon turmeric

1 teaspoon paprika

1 teaspoon ground cinnamon

6–8 boneless, skinless chicken breast halves (about 3 pounds), trimmed of fat
    and membrane and pounded to an even thickness

1½ teaspoons kosher salt

½ teaspoon black pepper

1 tablespoon olive oil

1 cup black Kalamata olives

2 lemons, thinly sliced

TO PREPARE THE MARINADE: Combine all the ingredients in a large bowl, or in a resealable plastic bag, and mix well. Add the chicken pieces and mix again. Cover or seal and refrigerate at least 4 hours and up to 2 days.

Sprinkle the chicken with the salt and pepper.

Place a large nonstick or cast-iron skillet over high heat and when it is hot, add the olive oil. Add the chicken breasts one at a time, allowing the pan to reheat for about 30 seconds between additions. Cook until the chicken is deeply browned and the juices run clear, 3–5 minutes per side, depending on the thickness. You will probably need to cook the chicken in two batches.

Serve immediately, garnished with the olives and lemon slices.

Coconut Spice Chicken

Sweet and spicy, this easy-to-make, wonderfully aromatic dish is best served with a green salad that's packed with fresh fruit and drizzled with Curried Dressing (page 69).

Although CORIANDER SEEDS come from the same plant as cilantro (which is the leaf), coriander and cilantro taste totally different and have very different uses. Lemony, sage-y and fragrant, coriander is most often used for pickling and in baked goods.

SERVES 6–8

For the marinade:

1 tablespoon olive oil
1 tablespoon ground coriander seed
1 tablespoon ground cumin
1 tablespoon Hungarian paprika
2 teaspoons light brown sugar

6–8 boneless, skinless chicken breast halves (about 3 pounds),
    trimmed of fat and membrane and pounded to an even
    thickness
1½ teaspoons kosher salt
½ teaspoon black pepper
1–2 tablespoons olive oil
3 tablespoons sweetened shredded coconut
2 limes, quartered

TO MAKE THE MARINADE: Place the olive oil, coriander, cumin, paprika and brown sugar in a large mixing bowl, or in a resealable plastic bag, and mix to combine. Add the chicken and mix again. Cover or seal, and refrigerate at least ½ hour and up to overnight. (You can freeze it at this point.)

Sprinkle the chicken with the salt and pepper.

Place a large nonstick or cast-iron skillet over high heat and when it is hot, add the oil. Add the chicken breasts one at a time, allowing the pan to reheat for about 30 seconds between additions. Cook until the chicken is deeply browned and the juices run clear, 3–5 minutes per side, depending on the thickness. You will probably need to cook the chicken in two batches.

Transfer the chicken to a platter, sprinkle with the coconut, and serve immediately, garnished with lime quarters.

Curried Chicken with Raisins and Cashews

This dish offers the flavor of a complicated curry dish without all the effort. Part of its appeal is in customizing each portion by adding the accompaniments at the end. You don't have to provide them all, so feel free to pick and choose as you like.

Serve the curry with steamed white rice, either on the side or as a bed underneath, and a green salad. The chicken can also be served cold, thinly sliced, on a bed of greens or in a sandwich.

> "Chutney is marvelous. I'm mad about it. To me, it's very imperial."
> —DIANA VREELAND, FASHION EDITOR (1903–1989)

SERVES 6–8

1½ cups buttermilk

2 garlic cloves, chopped or pressed

3 tablespoons curry powder

1½ teaspoons ground ginger

2 teaspoons ground cinnamon

¼ teaspoon cayenne pepper

6–8 boneless, skinless chicken breast halves (about 3 pounds), trimmed
     of fat and membrane, pounded to an even thickness

1½ teaspoons kosher salt

1 tablespoon olive oil

Optional accompaniments for serving:

½ cup chopped fresh cilantro leaves

¾ cup lightly toasted chopped cashews (page 12)

½ cup raisins

¼ cup unsweetened shredded coconut

½ bunch scallions, cut diagonally into 1-inch pieces

½–1 cup chutney (any kind is fine)

Place the buttermilk, garlic, curry powder, ginger, cinnamon and cayenne in a medium-size bowl, or in a resealable plastic bag, and mix well. Add the chicken and mix again. (The chicken can be frozen at this point.) Cover or seal, and refrigerate 4 hours and up to overnight.

Drain the chicken, discarding the marinade, and pat it dry with paper towels.

Sprinkle the chicken with the salt. Place a large nonstick or cast-iron skillet over high heat and when it is hot, add the olive oil. Add the chicken breasts one at a time, allowing the pan to reheat for about 30 seconds between additions. Cook until the chicken is deeply browned and the juices run clear, 3–5 minutes per side, depending on the thickness. You will probably need to cook the chicken in two batches.

Serve immediately, with any or all of the suggested accompaniments in small bowls.

Chicken Fajitas

Great for an informal dinner group, or for teens or kids, this recipe allows everyone to have a slightly different meal. You could also substitute an equal amount of thinly sliced flank steak.

SERVES 8

For the chicken:

3 pounds boneless, skinless chicken breasts, trimmed of fat and membrane,
    pounded to an even thickness and cut into thin strips
2 garlic cloves, minced
½ large red onion, coarsely chopped
½ cup chopped fresh cilantro leaves
⅓ cup fresh lime juice
2 tablespoons canola or vegetable oil
½–1 teaspoon crushed red pepper flakes

12–16 flour tortillas
2 tablespoons olive oil
2–3 red onions, halved and thinly sliced
2–3 red, orange or yellow bell peppers, thinly sliced
1 teaspoon kosher salt
½ teaspoon black pepper

For the accompaniments:

Sour cream or yogurt
Chopped avocado or Guacamole (page 28)
Salsa, store-bought or homemade

TO MARINATE THE CHICKEN: Place the chicken strips in a medium-size shallow glass or ceramic bowl, or in a resealable plastic bag. Add the garlic, onion, cilantro, lime juice, canola oil and red pepper flakes and mix to combine. Cover or seal, and refrigerate at least 1 hour and up to 4 hours.

Preheat the oven to 250 degrees.

Wrap the tortillas in aluminum foil, place them on a baking sheet and transfer to the oven to keep warm.

Place a large nonstick or cast-iron skillet over medium-high heat and when it is hot, add 1 tablespoon olive oil. Add the onions and peppers and cook until they begin to soften and brown, 10–15 minutes. Place the vegetables on the baking sheet in the oven.

Drain the chicken, discarding the marinade, and pat dry with a paper towel. Sprinkle the chicken with the salt and pepper.

Reheat the skillet over high heat and when it is hot, add the remaining 1 tablespoon olive oil. Add the chicken strips, one at a time, allowing the pan to reheat for about 5 seconds between additions. Cook until the chicken is deeply browned and the juices run clear, 1–2 minutes per side, depending on the thickness of the pieces. You will probably need to cook the chicken in two batches. Remove the onions and peppers from the oven and transfer to a small serving bowl. Remove the tortillas from the oven and transfer to a platter.

Serve buffet style, chicken in the skillet and the sour cream, avocado and salsa on separate plates or bowls, allowing each person to assemble their own fajita.

Chicken Pot Pie

Old-fashioned, straightforward, country comfort food.

The quantities in this recipe are odd, but for good reason. The crust makes enough for one pie but the filling enough for four. I can't imagine that you have enough room in your freezer for three or four pies, but you probably have the room for the *filling* of three or four pies. Plus, if you're going to the trouble of making the filling, you might as well make enough for next time. You can also freeze the filling in individual portions and not even top them: my daughter, Lauren, likes the filling so much that sometimes she just heats it up in a bowl for lunch.

When you are cutting up the chicken and vegetables, be sure to make them all the same size.

> "That's something I've noticed about food: whenever there's a crisis if you can get people to eating normally things get better."
> —MADELEINE L'ENGLE, WRITER (B. 1918)

ONE PIE SERVES ABOUT 6

For the pastry (makes 1 double-crust pie):

3 cups all-purpose flour
1 teaspoon kosher salt
1 cup unsalted butter, chilled, cut into 1-inch pieces
½ cup cold water

For the filling (enough for 4 pies):

2 tablespoons unsalted butter
6–8 garlic cloves, chopped
2 cups chopped carrots

1 Spanish onion, halved and chopped

2 cups chopped celery

2 cups diced unpeeled potatoes

8 cups Chicken Stock (page 8)

1 tablespoon dried thyme

½ tablespoon dried sage

½ tablespoon dried rosemary

½ cup all-purpose flour

4 cups cooked chicken (I prefer white meat, but either dark
or white will work fine)

2 cups frozen peas

1 teaspoon kosher salt

½ teaspoon black pepper

For the egg wash:

1 large egg
2 tablespoons water

TO PREPARE THE PASTRY: Place the flour and salt in the bowl of a stand mixer fitted with a paddle and turn it to medium speed. Add the butter and mix until it resembles coarse sand, about 2 minutes. Add the water and mix until the dough just comes together, less than 1 minute. Divide the dough in half and shape each half into a disk. Wrap each disk in plastic wrap, or place it in a resealable plastic bag, and refrigerate at least 1 hour and up to overnight.

TO PREPARE THE FILLING: Place a large, heavy-bottomed pot over medium-high heat and when it is hot, add 1 tablespoon butter. When the butter has melted, add the garlic, carrots, onion and celery and cook until tender, 10–15 minutes. Add the potatoes and stir to combine. Add 6 cups chicken stock. Stir in the thyme, sage and rosemary and bring to a boil. Lower the heat to low and simmer until the potatoes are tender, 15–20 minutes. Remove from the heat.

(Continued on next page)

Place the remaining 1 tablespoon butter in a small pot over medium heat and when it has melted, add the flour and stir to form a thick paste. Continue stirring to cook out the raw flour flavor of the roux, 2–3 minutes. Add the remaining 2 cups chicken stock and bring to a boil, stirring constantly. Continue cooking until the mixture is very thick and smooth, 3–5 minutes. Add this mixture to the stew pot and bring to one quick boil. Remove from heat and add the chicken, peas, salt and pepper. Set aside for 15 minutes. Pour into a shallow dish and refrigerate covered, at least 2 hours and up to 8.

While the chicken mixture is cooling, roll out the crusts: Remove one disk of pie dough from the refrigerator. Roll it out to an even ⅛-inch thickness on a well-floured surface. Place it in a 9-inch deep-dish pie pan, leaving at least ½ inch of overhang. Refrigerate. Repeat with the second disk, but place the rolled-out dough on a lightly floured sheet pan or plate, cover with plastic wrap or waxed paper and refrigerate.

When the chicken mixture is cold, pour it into the pie pan. Top with the second crust. Trim the edges and tuck the overhang under, forming a thick edge. Crimp decoratively as desired, and cut several slits in the top crust to ventilate.

TO MAKE THE EGG WASH: Place the egg and water in a small bowl and mix well. Brush the mixture over the top crust. (The pie can be refrigerated up to 2 days or frozen for 2 months.)

Preheat the oven to 375 degrees.

Place the pie on a baking sheet and transfer it to the oven. Bake until the crust is browned and the pie is heated throughout, 35–45 minutes. Set aside to cool 5–10 minutes before serving.

Whole Chicken and Chicken Breasts

Brine for Chicken

Brine is a saltwater solution, sometimes with added sugar, spices or herbs. A brined whole or cut up (bone-in) chicken is a better chicken. Whether you are going to make the plainest chicken breasts or something more complex, if you brine first, you'll have a plumper, moister, tastier chicken.

If you want, you can add herbs and spices to this brine: If you are making curried chicken, add 1 tablespoon curry; if tarragon is in the recipe, add 1 tablespoon tarragon; and so on.

½ cup kosher salt
2 tablespoons white or light brown sugar
2 cups boiling water
4–7 pounds whole chicken or chicken parts

If you are using a whole chicken, remove and discard the giblets and neck.

Rinse the chicken in several changes of cold water.

Place the salt, sugar and boiling water in a small bowl and mix until the salt and sugar are dissolved.

Place the chicken in a gallon-size resealable plastic bag or other large container. Cover with cold water, and when the chicken is fully immersed, slowly add the saltwater, stirring as you add it. Cover or seal, and refrigerate at least 1 hour and up to 8.

(Continued on next page)

Remove the chicken from the brine and rinse it well with cold water.

TO AIR DRY: Place the chicken, uncovered, in the refrigerator for at least 1 hour and up to 8 hours (this will help the skin crisp).

Proceed with your recipe.

Roasted Chicken with Variations

It doesn't get more basic or more delectable than a perfectly roasted chicken. Consider making two; the leftovers are fantastic.

> "The ambition of every good cook must be to make something very good with the fewest possible ingredients."
>
> —URBAIN DUBOIS, CHEF (1818-1901)

SERVES 4

1 whole roaster chicken, about 5 pounds, brined (page 155) and dried
2 teaspoons olive oil
1½ teaspoons kosher salt
¼ teaspoon black pepper
1 lemon, halved

Preheat the oven to 425 degrees.

Rub the chicken skin and flesh with the olive oil, and sprinkle with the salt and pepper. Squeeze the lemon juice over the chicken and place the halves in the cavity.

Place the chicken on a rack in a roasting pan. Cook until the juices run clear from the breast and the leg moves easily, about 1¼ hours. Do not baste.

Option One

  3 garlic cloves, thinly sliced
  2 tablespoons fresh rosemary or 2 teaspoons dried rosemary

Gently lift the skin and place the garlic slices and rosemary under it. Rub the chicken with olive oil and proceed as described.

Option Two

Add a generous sprinkling of paprika with the salt and pepper.

Option Three

  2 ripe pears (any kind will do), peeled and diced
  1 butternut squash, peeled and cut into 1-inch cubes
  ½ cup water or Chicken Stock (page 8)
  ½–1 cup dry vermouth or dry white wine

After placing the chicken on the rack, surround it with the pears and squash. Pour the water or stock and vermouth into the roasting pan.

Option Four

  12–16 small new potatoes, halved or quartered
  2 red onions, peeled, keeping root intact, cut into 8 wedges
  ½ cup dry white vermouth or dry white wine

After placing the chicken on the rack, surround it with the potatoes and onions. Pour the vermouth into the roasting pan.

Spice-Rubbed Chicken Breasts

Try this deeply flavored seasoning paste on sirloin steak too.

> "There is no sight on earth more appealing than the sight of a woman making dinner for someone she loves."
>
> —THOMAS WOLFE, WRITER (1900–1938)

SERVES 6–8

2 tablespoons olive oil

2 tablespoons chili powder

1 teaspoon garlic powder

2 teaspoons ground cumin

½ teaspoon black pepper

1 teaspoon ground cinnamon

6 pounds bone-in, skin-on chicken breasts (about 6–8), halved and
    trimmed of excess fat

Place the olive oil, chili powder, garlic powder, cumin, pepper and cinnamon in a large bowl, or in a resealable plastic bag, and mix to combine. Add the chicken breasts and mix well. Cover or seal, and refrigerate at least overnight and up to 2 days. (The chicken can be frozen at this point.)

Preheat the oven to 450 degrees.

Transfer the chicken to a 9 x 13-inch baking pan, place it in the oven and cook until the chicken is deeply browned and cooked throughout, about 45 minutes. Serve immediately, or cover and refrigerate up to 2 days.

Citrus Chicken with Oregano and Cumin

This recipe calls for a lot of citrus zesting, which takes time but is well worth it (and much easier if you use a Microplane).

Fine-grained rasps that were originally used as woodworking tools, MICROPLANES are indispensable for zesting citrus fruits. I know lots of people who use them for garlic, ginger, nuts, Parmesan cheese and even chocolate.

> "Be who you are and say what you feel, because those who mind don't matter, and those who matter don't mind."
>
> —THEODOR SEUSS GEISEL, WRITER (1904–1991)

SERVES 6–8

2 tablespoons vegetable or olive oil

2 tablespoons dried oregano

2 teaspoons ground cumin

4 garlic cloves, minced

Grated zest and juice of 2 limes or lemons

Grated zest and juice of 2 oranges, or ½ cup orange juice

2 teaspoons kosher salt

1 teaspoon black pepper

6 pounds bone-in, skin-on, chicken breasts (about 6–8), halved and trimmed of excess fat

Place the vegetable oil, oregano, cumin, garlic, citrus zest and juice in a large nonreactive bowl or a resealable plastic bag, and mix to combine. Add the chicken breasts and mix well.

Cover or seal, and refrigerate at least ½ hour and no longer than 1 hour.

Preheat the oven to 400 degrees.

Transfer the chicken to a 9 x 13-inch baking pan, place it in the oven and cook until the chicken is deeply browned and cooked throughout, about 45 minutes. Serve immediately, or cover and refrigerate up to 2 days.

Jamaican Jerk Chicken

There was a time when I made this chicken at least twice a week—and I always made enough so that I would have cold leftovers for a few days. (I guess that means I ate it every day!) There is something both seductive and addictive about this heady, aromatic, and spicy combination of flavors.

Serve the chicken with a salad of cucumber and chopped red onion, dressed with cider vinegar and a pinch of sugar.

CHINESE FIVE-SPICE POWDER is a combination of ground anise, star anise, cinnamon, cloves, fennel and sometimes black pepper, usually in equal parts.

Also know as Jamaica pepper, the scent and flavor of ALLSPICE is reminiscent of cloves, pepper, cinnamon and nutmeg. It is actually the dried unripe berry of the pimento tree. If you don't have allspice berries, you can substitute ground allspice.

One of the fieriest of all chile peppers, the small lantern-shaped SCOTCH BONNET CHILE ranges in color from yellow to red to green. Be sure to use rubber gloves when preparing the peppers. For less heat, discard the seeds and ribs.

SERVES 6–8

- 2 Spanish onions, halved and chopped
- 6 medium scallions, chopped
- 6 Scotch bonnet chiles
- 4 garlic cloves, chopped
- 2 tablespoons five-spice powder
- 2 tablespoons allspice berries, coarsely ground
- 2 tablespoons black pepper
- 2 teaspoons dried thyme
- 2 teaspoons ground nutmeg
- 2 teaspoons kosher salt
- 1 cup soy sauce
- 6 pounds bone-in, skin-on chicken breasts (about 6–8), halved and trimmed of excess fat

Place the onions, scallions, chiles, garlic, five-spice powder, allspice, pepper, thyme, nutmeg, salt and soy sauce in a food processor fitted with a steel blade. Process well.

Place the chicken in a large nonreactive bowl or a resealable plastic bag and add the onion mixture. Mix well, cover or seal, and refrigerate at least overnight and up to 3 days. (The chicken can be frozen at this point.)

Preheat the oven to 400 degrees.

Transfer the chicken and the onion mixture to a large baking pan, place it in the oven and cook until the chicken is deeply browned and cooked through, about 45 minutes. Serve immediately, or cover and refrigerate up to 2 days.

Roasted Chicken with Artichokes, Lemon and Onions

An adaptation of my friend Lizzy Shaw's recipe, this is especially good for a dinner party. In fact, Lizzy has several friends who insist she make it when they come to her home. It can be completely assembled ahead of time, so you can spend time with your guests instead of being sequestered in the kitchen.

Serve the chicken with steamed rice or with Sautéed Rice with Spinach and Feta Cheese (page 124).

Do not substitute canned or marinated artichoke hearts for the frozen.

SERVES 6–8

6 pounds bone-in, skin-on chicken breasts, halved and trimmed of excess fat, or
    1 fryer chicken, 4–4½ pounds, cut into 8 pieces, plus
    1½–2 pounds any combination of chicken breasts, legs and thighs,
    trimmed of excess fat
¼ cup olive oil
5 garlic cloves, thinly sliced
1 tablespoon dried rosemary
1 tablespoon dried thyme
1 tablespoon dried oregano
2 teaspoons dried sage
1 tablespoon kosher salt
1 teaspoon black pepper
1 teaspoon crushed red pepper flakes or crushed dried chipotle chile flakes
    (optional)
Two 12-ounce bags frozen artichoke hearts
2 Spanish onions, peeled, keeping root intact, and cut into 8 wedges
3–4 lemons, thinly sliced

Preheat the oven to 425 degrees.

Place the chicken, olive oil, garlic, herbs, salt and pepper in a large bowl. Add the red pepper flakes, if desired, and mix well. Add the artichoke hearts (it's okay if they are still frozen), onions and lemons, and mix well. (The mixture can be covered and frozen up to 2 months.)

Transfer everything to a rimmed baking sheet and arrange the ingredients in a single layer. Place in the oven and bake until deeply browned and crispy, about 1 hour. Serve immediately.

Hunter's Chicken

Serve this savory stewlike dish with steamed white rice and steamed or roasted zucchini.

> "Ever consider what pets must think of us? I mean, here we come back
> from a grocery store with the most amazing haul—chicken, pork, half a
> cow. They must think we're the greatest hunters on earth!"
>
> —ANNE TYLER, WRITER (B. 1941)

SERVES 6–8

6 pounds bone-in, skin-on chicken breasts, halved and trimmed of excess fat, or
    1 fryer chicken, 4–4½ pounds, cut into 8 pieces, plus
    1½–2 pounds any combination of breasts, legs and thighs,
    trimmed of excess fat
1 tablespoon kosher salt
1 teaspoon black pepper
1 tablespoon canola, safflower or olive oil
1 large Spanish or yellow onion, halved and sliced
4 garlic cloves, chopped, pressed or thinly sliced
3 celery stalks, chopped
4–5 carrots, chopped
2 red, yellow or orange bell peppers, chopped
1¼ pounds button mushrooms, halved
½–1 ounce dried porcini mushrooms, chopped (optional)
1 tablespoon chopped fresh thyme or 1–2 teaspoons dried thyme
1 tablespoon chopped fresh rosemary or 1–2 teaspoons dried rosemary
Two 16-ounce cans diced tomatoes, undrained
1 cup Chicken Stock (page 8)

Sprinkle the chicken with the salt and pepper. Place a large nonstick or cast-iron
skillet over medium-high heat and when it is hot, add the oil. Add the chicken, one

piece at a time, and cook until well browned, 3–4 minutes on each side. You will need to do this in two or three batches. Remove the chicken from the pan and set aside.

While the chicken is cooking, place a large Dutch oven over medium-high heat and add some of the fat from the skillet. When it is hot, add the onion, garlic, celery, carrots, bell peppers, both mushrooms and the herbs. Cook until the vegetables soften, 10–15 minutes. Add the tomatoes and chicken stock and bring to a boil. Add the browned chicken and cook over the lowest possible heat for 1 hour, partially covered, stirring occasionally.

Serve immediately or transfer to a container or a resealable plastic bag, cover or seal, and refrigerate up to 2 days.

Chicken Fricassee

This time-honored French dish is a little fussy but worth the effort. Although I am almost violently opposed to using two pots when making what is essentially a one-pot dish, in this case it really makes sense.

A FRICASSEE **is a dish of meat (usually chicken) that has been sautéed in butter and then stewed with vegetables.**

SERVES 6–8

6 pounds bone-in, skin-on chicken breasts, halved and trimmed of excess fat, or
    1 fryer chicken, 4–4½ pounds, cut into 8 pieces, plus
    1½–2 pounds any combination of breasts, legs and thighs,
    trimmed of excess fat
1½ teaspoons kosher salt
1 teaspoon black pepper
1 tablespoon unsalted butter
1 large Spanish onion, halved and sliced
4 garlic cloves, thinly sliced
4 celery stalks, cut in thick julienne
1 pound carrots, cut in thick julienne
1 pound button mushrooms, sliced or chopped
1½ teaspoons dried thyme
2 bay leaves
5 tablespoons all-purpose flour
1 cup dry white vermouth
5 cups Chicken Stock (page 8)
2 tablespoons heavy cream (optional)
2 tablespoons fresh lemon juice
2 teaspoons fresh thyme leaves
¼ cup chopped fresh Italian flat-leaf parsley leaves

Sprinkle the chicken with the salt and pepper. Place a large nonstick or cast-iron skillet over medium-high heat and when it is hot, add the butter. Add the chicken, one piece at a time, waiting about 30 seconds between additions, and cook until well browned, 3–4 minutes on each side. You will have to do this in two or three batches. Remove the chicken from the skillet and set aside.

While the chicken is cooking, place a large Dutch oven over medium-high heat, add 1 tablespoon fat from the skillet, and when it is hot, add the onion, garlic, celery, carrots, mushrooms, dried thyme and bay leaves. Cook until the carrots begin to soften, 10–15 minutes. Sprinkle the flour over the vegetables, 1 tablespoon at a time, stirring vigorously all the while.

When the flour has been completely incorporated, gradually add the vermouth and the chicken stock. Add the browned chicken and cook, partially covered, over the lowest possible heat for 1–1½ hours, stirring occasionally.

Serve immediately, or transfer to a container or a resealable plastic bag, cover or seal, and refrigerate up to 2 days. Just prior to serving, remove the bay leaves. Add the cream and lemon juice and cook until heated through. Garnish with the fresh thyme and parsley.

Chicken Marbella

Over the years I've made many variations of the famous Chicken Marbella recipe from *The Silver Palate Cookbook*. Here's the most current version in my repertoire.

SERVES 6-8

6 pounds bone-in, skin-on chicken breasts, halved and trimmed of excess fat, or

    1 fryer chicken, 4–4½ pounds, cut into 8 pieces, plus

    1½–2 pounds any combination of breasts, legs and thighs,

    trimmed of excess fat

⅔ cup olive or canola oil

⅔ cup red wine vinegar

¼ cup dried oregano

2 tablespoons chopped garlic

3 bay leaves

2 cups green olives (any kind is fine), pimento removed if stuffed

24 dried pitted prunes

24 dried apricots

12 dried figs

1 cup dry white wine

1 cup light brown sugar

1 teaspoon kosher salt

Place the chicken, olive oil, vinegar, oregano, garlic and bay leaves in a large bowl and mix well. Transfer to a resealable plastic bag and refrigerate at least overnight and up to 2 days. (The chicken can be frozen at this point.)

Preheat the oven to 425 degrees.

Transfer the chicken and marinade to a large bowl and add all the remaining ingredients. Stir to mix.

Transfer everything to a rimmed baking sheet and arrange the ingredients in a single layer. Place in the oven and bake until deeply browned and crispy, about 1 hour. Remove the bay leaves and serve immediately.

Thanksgiving: Roasted Turkey and Everything Else

The first time I ever made Thanksgiving dinner was for my brand-new-in-laws. I made a very exotic lobster dish over a stew of lentils du Puy.

I made all sorts of wonderful side dishes and a fairly esoteric dessert. My ex-husband and I spent hours and hours on these dishes and plenty of money. We figured we'd impress his parents with my culinary prowess, assuming they'd had enough turkey, stuffing and mashed potatoes to last a lifetime.

Wrong. They stared at the food, confused. They clearly thought that this meal, while delicious, was certainly odd.

The next year I made turkey, to the delight of all. This time we invited his parents, my parents and all extended family. Whenever I deviate too much from the traditional, I get into trouble, so I have decided Thanksgiving is not where I'll showcase my creativity.

The Turkey

TURKEY TIPS: **Clean your oven!**

You can use any roasting pan, including a disposable one. If you use a disposable pan, make sure to put it on a large, sturdy baking sheet.

DEFROSTING: It takes about 1 day for every 4 pounds of turkey. Do the math! If you have missed the deadline, at least a full day before (so you aren't worrying about it overnight), place the turkey, it in its original wrapping, in a bucket or sink of cold water and leave it for about 10 hours or about 30 minutes per pound. Butterball recommends that you change the water every half hour. If you haven't started the process the day before, either get a fresh turkey or order out.

1 turkey, 12–22 pounds
2 medium onions, coarsely chopped
2–3 carrots, coarsely chopped
2 celery stalks, coarsely chopped
1 lemon, quartered
2 rosemary branches, 4½–5½ inches long, or 2 thyme sprigs, 3–4 inches long
¼ cup unsalted butter, melted
2 teaspoons kosher salt
1 teaspoon black pepper
1 cup water

Place one oven rack in the lowest position and remove the remaining racks. Preheat the oven to 425 degrees.

Line a 12-inch V-shaped roasting rack with aluminum foil. Poke holes in the foil with the tip of a skewer or knife. Place the rack in a large shallow roasting pan.

Remove the giblets (neck, heart and gizzard) and set them aside to make the gravy (page 172). Discard the liver. Rinse the turkey several times, inside and out, with cold running water. Thoroughly pat dry with paper towels; the turkey skin should be as dry as possible.

Place the onions, carrots, celery, lemon quarters and rosemary in a medium-size bowl and toss to combine. Set aside.

Brush the turkey breast with 2 tablespoons butter; then sprinkle with 1 teaspoon salt and ½ teaspoon pepper. Set the turkey, *breast-side down,* on the prepared rack. Brush the turkey back with the remaining 2 tablespoons butter, and sprinkle with the remaining 1 teaspoon salt and ½ teaspoon pepper. Fill the cavity with half the onion mixture. Scatter the remaining mixture in the roasting pan; pour the water over the vegetables.

Transfer the pan to the oven and cook for 1 hour. Remove the roasting pan from the oven and transfer it to a countertop; close the oven door. Do not place the turkey on the oven door! Lower the temperature to 325 degrees.

Using a clean dish towel or two pot holders, turn the turkey over so it is breast-side up in the rack. Return the roasting pan to the oven and cook until the dark thigh meat registers 170–180 degrees, the legs move freely and the juices run clear (not pinkish red), 2–3 hours depending on the size of the bird. Remove from the oven and let rest, uncovered, for about 20 minutes. Throw the dish towel in the laundry.

"Most turkeys taste better the day after. My mother's tasted better the day before."

—RITA RUDNER, COMEDIAN (B. 1955)

Pan Gravy

This is the best gravy in the entire world. It *is* on the thin side, so if you absolutely must have a thick gravy, add a little more flour, but know that it will muddy the great flavor. Start the gravy when the bird goes in the oven.

YIELD: ABOUT 9 CUPS

1 tablespoon olive or canola oil
Turkey giblets, neck and tail piece
1 Spanish onion, unpeeled, chopped
9 cups turkey broth or Chicken Stock (page 8) or 6 cups canned
    low-sodium chicken broth plus 3 cups water
2 fresh thyme sprigs
8 fresh Italian flat-leaf parsley stems
⅓ cup unsalted butter
¼ cup plus 2 tablespoons all-purpose flour
1½ cups dry white wine
Kosher salt and black pepper

Place a large heavy-bottomed skillet over medium-high heat and when it is hot, add the oil. Add the turkey giblets, neck and tail and cook until golden brown, about 5 minutes. Add the onion and cook, stirring occasionally, until softened, about 3 minutes. Lower the heat to low, cover and cook until the turkey parts and the onion release their juices, about 20 minutes. Raise the heat to high, add the stock and herbs and bring to a boil. Lower the heat to low and simmer, uncovered, skimming any scum that may rise to the surface, until the broth is rich and flavorful, about 30 minutes.

Pour the broth through a strainer into a bowl. Discard all the solids except the heart and gizzard. You should have 7–8 cups liquid. When it is cool enough to handle, remove the gristle from the gizzard; then dice the heart and gizzard. Transfer the broth to a medium-size saucepan and bring just to a boil over medium heat.

Place the butter in a large heavy-bottomed saucepan over medium-low heat and when it has melted, very slowly whisk in the flour to make a roux. Cook slowly, stirring constantly, until it is nut brown and fragrant, about 10 minutes. Vigorously whisk all but 1 cup of the hot broth into the roux. Raise the heat to medium-high and bring to a boil. Then lower the heat to medium-low and simmer, stirring occasionally, until slightly thickened and flavorful, about 30 minutes. Set aside until the turkey is done.

While the turkey is resting, spoon out and discard as much fat as possible from the roasting pan, leaving behind the caramelized herbs and vegetables. Place the roasting pan over two burners at medium-high heat (if the drippings are not dark brown, cook, stirring constantly, until they caramelize).

Return the gravy to a simmer over medium heat. Add the wine to the roasting pan and scrape up the browned bits clinging to the bottom; boil until reduced by half, about 5 minutes. Add the remaining 1 cup broth to the roasting pan, and then strain this mixture into the gravy, pressing on the solids in the strainer to extract as much liquid as possible. Stir in the diced giblets and return to a simmer. Add salt and pepper to taste. Use immediately, cover and refrigerate up to 2 days, or freeze up to 2 months.

Corn Bread Stuffing

> "No more turkey, but I'd like some more of the bread it ate."
> —HANK KETCHAM, CARTOONIST (1920–2001)

YIELD: ABOUT 10 CUPS

2 leeks

2 teaspoons olive oil or unsalted butter

4 celery stalks, diced

3 Granny Smith apples, peeled if desired, and diced

7–8 cups crumbled day-old corn bread, store-bought or homemade from your favorite recipe

1 cup chopped, lightly toasted walnuts, pecans or hazelnuts (page 12)

3 tablespoons chopped fresh Italian flat-leaf parsley leaves

3 tablespoons chopped fresh sage leaves or 1 tablespoon dried sage

3 tablespoons chopped fresh rosemary leaves or 1 tablespoon dried rosemary

3 tablespoons chopped fresh thyme leaves or 1 tablespoon dried thyme

1 teaspoon kosher salt

¼ cup dry vermouth

2 large eggs

½–1 cup Chicken Stock (page 8) or apple juice

Preheat the oven to 350 degrees. Lightly butter a 9 x 13-inch pan.

Trim the roots off the leeks and remove all but 2 inches of the green part. Dice the remaining portion and wash in several changes of hot water, being sure to get rid of any sand; drain well in a colander.

Place a large skillet over low heat and when it is hot, add the oil. Add the leeks, celery and apples and cook until tender, 15–20 minutes.

Add all the remaining ingredients and toss well. Place the stuffing in the prepared pan and transfer to the oven. Cook until golden brown on top, about 35 minutes.

Sydny's Cranberry Chutney

This chutney is great for Thanksgiving but it's also good on a turkey burger (pages 180–184), as an accompaniment to Roasted Chicken (page 156), as a spread for turkey or chicken sandwiches or even mixed into cream cheese for a dip.

YIELD: ABOUT 2 CUPS

One 12-ounce bag cranberries (3 cups)
¼ cup orange juice
1–2 jalapeño or chipotle chiles, minced
½ cup light brown sugar
½ teaspoon kosher salt
Grated zest of 1 lime
Grated zest of 1 orange
¾ cup lightly toasted pecans or walnuts (page 12), coarsely chopped

Place the cranberries, orange juice, chiles and brown sugar in a small saucepan and cook over medium-high heat until the cranberries are soft and have absorbed all the liquid, about 10 minutes. Set aside to cool.

Stir in the salt, lime and orange zests and nuts. Serve immediately, or cover and refrigerate for up to 2 weeks.

Nancy's Raw Cranberry Relish

Here's a fresh alternative to traditional cranberry sauce. Make this relish with half a big bag of cranberries and use the other half to make either the recipe on the bag or Sydny's Cranberry Chutney (page 175).

> "A little nonsense now and then is relished by the wisest men."
> —ROALD DAHL, WRITER (1916–1990)

YIELD: ABOUT 3½–4 CUPS

4½ cups cranberries
2 oranges, peeled and diced
2 red apples, diced
½ cup sugar

Place everything in the bowl of a food processor fitted with a steel blade and pulse until finely chopped. Cover and refrigerate at least one hour and up to overnight.

Mashed Sweet Potatoes with Crunchy Pecan Topping

Sweet potatoes are one of my most beloved vegetables, and it practically makes me delirious to know that they are so good for you, too. Rich in fiber and beta-carotene, sweet potatoes are also high in both calcium and potassium.

The sweet potatoes can be prepared up to two days ahead, but don't add the topping until you are ready to bake them.

SERVES 8–12

8 sweet potatoes, cut in large dice

1⅓ cups pecans, finely chopped

1 cup light brown sugar, spread out on a plate and left overnight to dry

½ cup unsalted butter, at room temperature

¼ cup maple syrup

2 teaspoons kosher salt

½–1 teaspoon black pepper

Place the sweet potatoes in a large pot, cover with water and bring to a boil over high heat. Reduce the heat to medium-low and cook until the potatoes are tender and all but 1 inch of the water has evaporated, about 20 minutes.

While the sweet potatoes are cooking, place the pecans and brown sugar in a small bowl and mix until well combined. Set aside.

Preheat the oven to 350 degrees.

Transfer the sweet potatoes and remaining water to a food processor fitted with a steel blade and process until smooth. Add the butter, maple syrup, salt and pepper, and mix until combined. Transfer to a 9 x 13-inch baking pan and top with the pecan and brown sugar mixture. Place in the oven and bake until golden brown, about 30 minutes.

Lemon Sweet Potatoes

Honestly I dreamed of these: sweet, tart and oh-so-lemon-y, these are sooooo good I could eat the whole batch myself.

SERVES 8–10

8 sweet potatoes, peeled, if desired, and cut in thick rounds
½ cup unsalted butter
I cup sugar
I cup water
I teaspoon kosher salt
Grated zest and juice of 2 lemons

Preheat the oven to 400 degrees.

Place the sweet potatoes in a 9 x 13-inch baking pan. Place the butter, sugar, water, salt and lemon zest and juice in a small saucepan and bring to a boil over high heat. Pour the sugar syrup over the sweet potatoes, cover with aluminum foil, transfer to the oven and bake for 30 minutes.

Remove the foil and pour all the liquid into a bowl. Pour the liquid back over the sweet potatoes, return the pan to the oven and cook, uncovered, until the sweet potatoes are caramelized and bubbly, about 30 additional minutes.

Ground Turkey

Turkey burgers are a versatile alternative to beef burgers, and their mild flavor helps them take on seasonings even better than beef. Light, low in fat and easy to make, turkey burgers are perfect for freezing in patties. Casual enough for weekdays, they can also be dressed up for a casual dinner party.

The following recipes can be doubled.

Be sure to AVOID FREEZER BURN (and sogginess) by double wrapping them: first in waxed paper and then in a resealable plastic bag. Defrost overnight in the fridge and be sure they are completely thawed before cooking.

Turkey Burgers with Feta and Herbs

My favorite cheeseburger has the cheese stuffed inside rather than melted on top. The first time I made a cheese-stuffed burger was in elementary school, when I had my first cookbook: I can't remember the name but it was written by Snoopy, the beagle made famous by Charles Schultz in the *Peanuts* cartoon. Snoopy's suggestion was to stuff the burger with cheddar cheese and chopped tomatoes. I remember eating a lot of burgers that first year. This one has Greek-inspired flavors; I don't think Snoopy would disapprove.

> "There are two types of mints you never turn down in life: breath mints and compliments. Either way, someone is trying to tell you something."
> —ANONYMOUS

SERVES 4

1¼–1½ pounds ground turkey
2 garlic cloves, minced
1 teaspoon Dijon mustard
¼–½ teaspoon black pepper
3 tablespoons chopped fresh mint leaves (optional)
2 teaspoons dried rosemary or 2 tablespoons chopped fresh rosemary leaves
2 tablespoons chopped fresh Italian flat-leaf parsley leaves
2 teaspoons dried oregano
⅛–¼ teaspoon cayenne pepper (optional)
4 tablespoons feta cheese
Kosher salt and black pepper to taste
1 lime, quartered

Place the turkey, garlic, mustard, pepper, mint, if desired, rosemary, parsley, oregano and cayenne, if desired, in a large mixing bowl and gently mix. Divide the mixture into 4 balls of equal size.

Divide each ball in half and flatten the halves. Place 1 tablespoon feta on each of 4 patties. Top them with the other halves and re-form into patties. Seal the edges by pinching them together, and flatten to about 1 inch thick. (The patties can be frozen at this point.)

Sprinkle with salt and pepper. Place a large nonstick or cast-iron skillet over medium-high heat and when it is very hot, add the burgers, allowing the pan to reheat for about 30 seconds between additions. Cook until deeply browned, 7–8 minutes on each side. Serve immediately, garnished with the lime quarters.

Todd's Turkey Burgers

When Todd English and I wrote *The Olives Table,* we included a recipe called Spicy Low Fat Chicken Patty, essentially a burger made out of well-chopped chicken plus spices. Using ground turkey, which wasn't so ubiquitous then, makes for far less fuss.

SERVES 4

1¼-1½ pounds ground turkey

⅓ red onion, finely chopped

½ cup chopped fresh cilantro leaves

3 garlic cloves, finely chopped

1 tablespoon finely chopped fresh gingerroot

1 teaspoon Dijon mustard

1–1½ teaspoons Vietnamese chili garlic sauce

1 teaspoon kosher salt

1 teaspoon black pepper

1–2 limes, quartered

Place the turkey, onion, cilantro, garlic, ginger, mustard and chili garlic sauce in a bowl and mix to combine. Divide the mixture into 4 balls of equal size, form into patties and flatten to about 1 inch thick.

Sprinkle with the salt and pepper. Place a large skillet over medium-high heat and when it is very hot, add the burgers, allowing the pan to reheat for about 30 seconds between additions. Cook until deeply browned, 7–8 minutes on each side. Serve immediately, garnished with the lime quarters.

Turkey Burgers with Indian Spices

A slightly exotic burger that's delicious served with thickened yogurt instead of ketchup. Roasted Potatoes (page 98) are the perfect accompaniment.

> "If you are ever at a loss to support a flagging conversation, introduce the subject of eating."
>
> —LEIGH HUNT, POET AND WRITER (1784–1859)

SERVES 4

1¼–1½ pounds ground turkey
4 garlic cloves, minced
2 tablespoons minced fresh gingerroot
Juice of 1 lime
1½ teaspoons ground cumin
1½ teaspoons black pepper
1½ teaspoons ground cinnamon
1½ teaspoons kosher salt
1 lime, quartered

Place the turkey, garlic, ginger, lime juice, cumin, pepper and cinnamon in a bowl and mix to combine. Divide the mixture into 4 balls of equal size, form into patties and flatten to about 1 inch thick.

Sprinkle with the salt. Place a large skillet over medium-high heat and when it is very hot, add the burgers, allowing the pan to reheat for about 30 seconds between additions. Cook until deeply browned, 7–8 minutes on each side. Serve immediately, garnished with the lime quarters.

Spicy Turkey Burgers with Chipotle Chiles

I don't know what I did before I discovered CHIPOTLES IN ADOBO SAUCE. Chipotles are smoked jalapeño peppers, and adobo is the herby, spicy, slightly vinegary tomato sauce they are packed in. They lend a wonderful warm and subtle-smoky heat to many dishes. Since I am always afraid of running out, I make sure to keep three or four cans of chipotles in adobo sauce in my pantry. Once you open the can, transfer the chipotles and the sauce to a small glass jar and refrigerate for up to three months.

SERVES 4

1¼–1½ pounds ground turkey
2–3 garlic cloves, minced
1 teaspoon Dijon mustard
1 teaspoon chili powder
1 teaspoon ground cumin
1 chipotle chile in adobo, chopped
2 teaspoons dried oregano
⅛–¼ teaspoon cayenne pepper (optional)
Kosher salt and black pepper to taste
1 lime, quartered

Combine all the ingredients except the salt, black pepper and lime in a large mixing bowl and gently mix. Divide the mixture into 4 balls of equal size, form into patties, and flatten to about 1 inch thick. Sprinkle with salt and pepper.

Place a large skillet over medium-high heat and when it is very hot, add the burgers, allowing the pan to reheat for about 30 seconds between additions. Cook until deeply browned, 7–8 minutes per side. Serve immediately, garnished with the lime quarters.

Meat

Strangely enough, I started eating more meat when I started shopping at warehouse clubs. Before that I had always made the same two meat dishes—Flank Steak with Soy Sauce, Sherry and Dijon Mustard (page 200) and Beef Chili (page 212)—and it wasn't until I had large quantities of meat on hand that I started to get creative. After being a vegetarian for ten years, I emerged an enthusiastic fan of beef.

Ground Beef

Traditional Meat Sauce

This is a classic meat sauce for pasta, which I especially like and use mostly for lasagna. Don't be tempted to shorten the cooking time—the long slow simmer makes a difference. You can substitute ground turkey or almost any kind of sausage, removed from the casing. If you use spicy sausage, reduce the herbs and spices by half. I've always made big batches of this sauce, but until I discovered the 102-ounce can, I resented the time I had to spend with the can opener.

TOMATO PASTE can be purchased in either a can or a tube. Since most recipes call for only a small amount, there is usually some left over if you use a can. Instead of just disposing of it, scoop out level tablespoons and place them at 1-inch intervals on plastic wrap. Place it in the freezer until the paste is solid, and then fold over the edges of the plastic wrap so that they cover the tomato paste. Place it in a resealable plastic bag and freeze for up to 4 months. Frozen tomato paste can be dropped directly into a hot dish.

> "When we win, I'm so happy I eat a lot. When we lose, I'm so depressed, I eat a lot. When we're rained out, I'm so disappointed I eat a lot."
>
> —TOMMY LASORDA, BASEBALL PITCHER AND MANAGER (B. 1927)

YIELD: ABOUT 14–16 CUPS

1 tablespoon olive oil

2 Spanish onions, halved and chopped

6–8 garlic cloves, chopped

1 tablespoon dried oregano

1 tablespoon dried basil

1 tablespoon fennel seed

½–1 teaspoon crushed red pepper flakes

2½ pounds ground beef

One 102-ounce can diced tomatoes (12 cups)

One 6-ounce can tomato paste

1 cup dry red wine

Place a large pot over medium heat and when it is hot, add the oil. Add the onions, garlic, herbs and red pepper flakes and cook until the onions are tender, 10–15 minutes.

Raise the heat to high and add the beef in four additions, each time breaking it up with a spoon. Cook just until it loses its rawness and begins to brown, about 5 minutes. Add the tomatoes, tomato paste and wine and bring just to a boil. Lower the heat to low and cook, covered, for 1 hour. Remove the cover and cook for 1 additional hour.

Serve immediately; cool, cover and refrigerate up to 5 days; or freeze in a resealable plastic bag up to 3 months.

Burgers au Poivre

This is a great burger for the pepper fanatic. Serve with Roasted Potatoes (page 98), Maple Syrup–Glazed Baby Carrots (page 92) and/or a tomato or green salad with blue cheese.

SERVES 6–8

2½ pounds ground beef
¼ cup coarsely ground black pepper
Grated zest of 2 lemons
1½ teaspoons kosher salt

Divide the beef into 6–8 balls and form into patties.

Place the pepper, lemon zest and salt on a plate and mix to combine. Dredge the patties in the mixture. (You can cover and freeze the patties up to 3 months.)

Place a large skillet over medium-high heat and when it is very hot, add the burgers, allowing the pan to reheat for 30 seconds between additions. Cook until deeply browned, 3–5 minutes on each side. Serve immediately.

Steak Tartare Burgers

This burger contains all the ingredients found in the traditional recipe for steak tartare—the classic dish of raw chopped meat, with all the flavor and none of the health risks. Serve with Roasted Potatoes (page 98) and/or a great big salad.

CAPERS are the unopened flower buds of the caper shrub, a creeping, weedlike, prickly perennial native to the Mediterranean. Why anyone first thought to eat a caper is not known, but they are mentioned as far back as the Old Testament; the Romans ate them with bread and used them to flavor sauces. Like fresh herbs, capers should be added at the end of cooking. While they have almost no nutritional value, they are thought to be an aphrodisiac, an antidepressant, and an appetite and digestive stimulant. They are always preserved, in either brine, salt or olive oil.

SERVES 6–8

2½ pounds ground beef

1 small red onion, halved and finely chopped (about 1 cup)

2 garlic cloves, finely chopped

¼ cup finely chopped fresh cilantro, basil and Italian flat-leaf parsley leaves, combined

2 tablespoons capers, rinsed (if packed in salt), drained and chopped

1 tablespoon plus 1 teaspoon Worcestershire sauce

1½ teaspoons Tabasco sauce

2 teaspoons Dijon mustard

Juice and grated zest of 1 lemon

1 teaspoon black pepper

1 teaspoon kosher salt

Place all the ingredients except the salt in a large bowl and mix until combined. Divide into 6–8 balls and form into patties. (You can cover and freeze the patties for up to 3 months.)

Sprinkle with the salt. Place a large skillet over medium-high heat and when it is very hot, add the burgers, allowing the pan to reheat for 30 seconds between additions. Cook until deeply browned, 3–5 minutes on each side. Serve immediately.

Barbecue Burgers

Instead of slathering a burger with barbecue sauce, the sauce ingredients are added directly to the ground beef. You can substitute ground pork, chicken, turkey, or a combination, for the beef. No need for ketchup with these burgers.

> "I like a cook who smiles out loud when he tastes his own work. Let God worry about your modesty; I want to see your enthusiasm."
> —ROBERT FARRAR CAPON, PRIEST AND AUTHOR (B. 1925)

SERVES 6–8

1 bunch scallions, chopped
Grated zest of ½ lemon
3 ounces tomato paste
2–3 garlic cloves, minced
1 tablespoon light brown sugar
1 tablespoon soy sauce
1 tablespoon chili powder
1 tablespoon Dijon mustard
1 teaspoon black pepper
2½ pounds ground beef
1½ teaspoons kosher salt
2 lemons or limes, quartered

Place all the ingredients except the beef, salt and lemon quarters in a large bowl and mix until combined. Add the beef and mix again. Divide into 6–8 patties. (You can cover and freeze the patties for up to 3 months.)

Sprinkle with the salt. Place a large skillet over medium-high heat and when it is very hot, add the burgers, allowing the pan to reheat for 30 seconds between additions. Cook until deeply browned, 3–5 minutes on each side. Serve immediately, garnished with the lemon quarters.

Burgers with Goat Cheese and Herbes de Provence

Here's a burger with a distinctly Mediterranean flair. Skip the usual soft bun and try this on a crusty French roll or tucked into pita bread. Serve with a salad of shredded romaine, scallions and dill, or with very ripe sliced tomatoes drizzled with olive oil.

HERBES DE PROVENCE is a mixture of savory, rosemary, cracked fennel seed, thyme, basil, tarragon, lavender and marjoram.

SERVES 6–8

2½ pounds ground beef
¾ cup goat or feta cheese, crumbled
3 tablespoons herbes de Provence
1 tablespoon kosher salt
¾ teaspoon black pepper

Divide the beef into 6–8 pieces of equal size. Divide each portion in half and flatten the halves. Place the cheese and herbes de Provence in a small bowl and mix well. Sprinkle half the patties with an equal amount of the cheese mixture. Top with the other halves and re-form into patties. Seal the edges by pinching them together, and flatten. (You can cover and freeze the patties for up to 3 months.)

Sprinkle with the salt and pepper. Place a large skillet over medium-high heat and when it is very hot, add the burgers, allowing the pan to reheat for 30 seconds between additions. Cook until deeply browned, 3–5 minutes on each side. Serve immediately.

Curried Cheddar Burgers with Chutney

The marriage of cheddar and chutney may seem unlikely, but it's truly delicious.

> "Cooking is at once one of the simplest and most gratifying of the arts, but to cook well one must love and respect food."
> —CRAIG CLAIBORNE, CHEF AND COOKBOOK AUTHOR (1920–2000)

SERVES 6-8

2½ pounds ground beef
½ pound sharp cheddar cheese, thinly sliced
½ cup mango chutney, store-bought or homemade (page 23)
1 tablespoon kosher salt
¾ teaspoon black pepper
1 tablespoon sugar
1½ tablespoons curry powder

Divide the beef into 6–8 pieces of equal size. Divide the portions in half and flatten the halves. Place an equal amount of cheese on half the patties, and top each with 1 tablespoon chutney. Top with the other halves and re-form into patties. Seal the edges by pinching them together, and flatten. (You can cover and freeze the patties for up to 3 months.)

Place the salt, pepper, sugar and curry powder on a plate and stir to mix. Just prior to cooking, lightly coat each patty with the mixture.

Place a large skillet over medium-high heat and when it is very hot, add the burgers, allowing the pan to reheat for 30 seconds between additions. Cook until deeply browned, 3–5 minutes on each side. Serve immediately.

Blackened Blue Burgers

Classic Cajun blackening spices coat these burgers stuffed with blue cheese. Of course you can eliminate the blue cheese or substitute smoked cheddar or Montrachet or another goat cheese.

> "Food for thought is no substitute for the real thing."
> —WALT KELLY, CARTOONIST (1913–1973)

SERVES 6–8

1 tablespoon dried oregano
2 teaspoons cayenne pepper
2 teaspoons black pepper
1 tablespoon garlic powder
1 tablespoon dried thyme
2 teaspoons Hungarian paprika
2 teaspoons kosher salt
2½ pounds ground beef
¾–1 pound blue cheese, crumbled or cut into 6–8 equal pieces

Preheat the broiler.

Place the oregano, peppers, garlic powder, thyme, paprika and salt on a plate, and stir to mix.

Divide the ground beef into 6–8 pieces of equal size. Divide each portion in half and form into patties. Place the blue cheese on half the patties, top with the other halves and re-form into patties. Seal the edges by pinching them together. Dredge the patties in the spice mixture. (You can cover and freeze the patties for up to 3 months.)

Place the patties on a broiler pan or baking sheet, set it about 2½–3 inches from the broiler and broil for 3–5 minutes per side (longer for well-done). Serve immediately.

Meat Loaf

This is comfort food at its best. Serve it with mashed potatoes (smooth or lumpy—it's up to you) and a green salad. You can also shape the meat into patties and make burgers if your family prefers. Leftover meat loaf makes wonderful sandwiches and crumbled, it can be added to beef chili.

> "The most remarkable thing about my mother is that for thirty years she served the family nothing but leftovers. The original meal has never been found."
>
> —CALVIN TRILLIN, WRITER (B. 1935)

SERVES 6–8

1 teaspoon olive oil

1 Spanish onion, halved and chopped

2–3 garlic cloves, finely chopped or pressed (optional)

2½ pounds ground beef

1½ cups Fresh Bread Crumbs (page 11)

3 large eggs, lightly beaten

1 cup tomato ketchup or barbecue sauce

½ cup chopped fresh Italian flat-leaf parsley leaves

¼ cup Dijon mustard

½ teaspoon kosher salt

1 teaspoon black pepper

Preheat the oven to 350 degrees.

Place a large skillet over medium heat and when it is hot, add the oil. Add the onion and garlic, if desired, and cook until golden, about 10 minutes. Set aside to cool.

Place the ground beef, bread crumbs, eggs, ¾ cup ketchup, parsley, mustard, salt and pepper in a bowl. Mix *by hand* until everything is thoroughly incorporated. Add the cooled onion mixture and mix again.

Divide the mixture in half and form into two logs. Spoon 2 tablespoons of the remaining ketchup over the top of each. (You can cover and freeze the meat loaves for up to 3 months.)

Place the loaves on a rimmed baking sheet, transfer to the oven and bake until the meat is cooked throughout and the tops are deeply browned, about 40 minutes. Let the meat loaf sit for a few minutes before slicing and serving.

Variations

TURKEY MEAT LOAF: Substitute an equal amount of ground turkey for the ground beef and add an extra egg.

A VARIATION ON BEEF MEAT LOAF: Try adding one of the following: ¼ cup prepared horseradish, or 4 slices chopped prosciutto, or 2 teaspoons Vietnamese chili garlic sauce.

Flank Steak and Steak Tips

Most flank steaks are too large for two people but not enough for four. Depending upon the recipe and how many people I'm serving, I often cook one and freeze the rest. It's certainly never worth the work to prepare only one.

In all the recipes, you can substitute steak tips for flank steak.

Flank Steak with Citrus, Soy and Garlic

This slightly Asian marinade is also great on chicken, salmon and pork. The red pepper flakes can be eliminated or reduced for a milder flavor.

Serve the steaks with mashed or Roasted Potatoes (page 98) and a green salad.

THE BEST WAY TO JUICE A LIME: Roll the lime around, pushing down on it with the palm of your hand. Then slice in half and juice.

SERVES 6

For the marinade:

Grated zest of 1 lime
⅓ cup orange juice, fresh or from concentrate
¼ cup fresh lime juice
3 tablespoons soy sauce
3 garlic cloves, finely chopped or pressed
1 tablespoon finely chopped fresh gingerroot
½ teaspoon crushed red pepper flakes

2 flank steaks (2¾–3½ pounds)
1½ teaspoons kosher salt
½ teaspoon black pepper

TO PREPARE THE MARINADE: Place the marinade ingredients in a small bowl and mix well. Place the steaks in a glass or ceramic bowl, or in a resealable plastic bag, and add the marinade. Cover or seal, and refrigerate at least 3 hours and up to overnight. Turn occasionally. (The steaks can be frozen up to 3 months.)

Preheat a grill or broiler.

Remove the steaks and discard the marinade. Sprinkle the steaks with the salt and pepper. Place them on a roasting pan or on a hot grill rack, and cook 4–5 minutes per side for medium-rare.

Transfer the steaks to a cutting board and thinly slice against the grain. Serve immediately.

Spicy Mustard Flank Steak

This robustly flavored steak is particularly tasty when grilled. I like to serve it with corn on the cob and potato salad.

> "Part of the secret of success in life is to eat what you like and let the food fight it out inside."
>
> —MARK TWAIN, HUMORIST, WRITER AND LECTURER (1835–1921)

SERVES 6

For the rub:

⅓ cup Dijon mustard
¾ teaspoon chili powder or chipotle chile powder
Juice of ½ lime
1½ teaspoons light brown sugar

2 flank steaks (2¾–3½ pounds)
1½ teaspoons kosher salt
½ teaspoon black pepper

TO MAKE THE RUB: Place the rub ingredients in a small bowl and mix well. Place the steaks in a glass or ceramic bowl, or in a resealable plastic bag, and add the rub, making sure the meat is thoroughly and evenly coated. Cover or seal, and refrigerate at least 3 hours and up to overnight. Turn occasionally. (The steaks can be frozen up to 3 months.)

Preheat a grill or broiler.

Remove the steaks and discard the leftover rub. Sprinkle the steaks with the salt and pepper. Place them on a roasting pan or on a hot grill rack, and cook 4–5 minutes per side for medium-rare.

Transfer the steaks to a cutting board and thinly slice against the grain. Serve immediately.

Mexican-Spiced Flank Steak

Sweet and spicy, this is best served with rice and roasted sweet potatoes. The marinade is also good on chicken and pork.

SERVES 6

For the marinade:

½–¾ teaspoon chili powder

2 teaspoons ground cumin

2 teaspoons dried oregano

2 garlic cloves, minced

1 tablespoon canola or olive oil

⅔ cup orange juice

2 tablespoons minced fresh cilantro leaves

2 flank steaks (2¾–3½ pounds)

1½ teaspoons kosher salt

½–1 teaspoon black pepper

TO PREPARE THE MARINADE: Place the marinade ingredients in a small bowl and mix well. Place the steaks in a glass or ceramic bowl or in a resealable plastic bag, and add the marinade. Cover or seal, and refrigerate at least 3 hours and up to overnight. Turn occasionally. (The steaks can be frozen up to 3 months.)

Preheat a grill or broiler.

Remove the steaks and discard the marinade. Sprinkle the steaks with the salt and pepper. Place them on a roasting pan or on a hot grill rack, and cook 4–5 minutes per side for medium-rare.

Transfer the steaks to a cutting board and thinly slice against the grain. Serve immediately.

Flank Steak with Soy Sauce, Sherry and Dijon Mustard

She probably doesn't even remember giving me this recipe, but my pal Susan Orlean sent me on my first foray into cooking flank steak twenty-five years ago. This marinade is also great on chicken and pork.

> "One should never refuse an invitation to lunch or dinner, for one never knows what one may have to eat the next day."
>
> —EDOUARD DE POMIANE, FOOD WRITER (1874–1964)

SERVES 6

For the marinade:

3 tablespoons soy sauce
3 tablespoons dry sherry
3 tablespoons Dijon mustard
¼ cup light brown sugar
1 tablespoon curry powder

2 flank steaks (2¾–3½ pounds)
½ teaspoon kosher salt
½ teaspoon black pepper

TO PREPARE THE MARINADE: Place the marinade ingredients in a small bowl and mix well. Place the steaks in a glass or ceramic bowl, or in a resealable plastic bag, and add the marinade. Cover or seal, and refrigerate at least 3 hours and up to overnight. Turn occasionally. (The steaks can be frozen up to 3 months.)

Preheat a grill or broiler.

Remove the steaks and discard the marinade. Sprinkle the steaks with the salt and pepper. Place them on a roasting pan or on a hot grill rack, and cook 4–5 minutes per side for medium-rare.

Transfer the steaks to a cutting board and thinly slice against the grain. Serve immediately.

Apricot Soy–Glazed Sirloin Steak Tips

A perfect combination of sweet, tart, spicy and rich. Serve this with sweet potatoes.

> "My weaknesses have always been food and men—in that order."
> —DOLLY PARTON, SINGER AND ACTRESS (B. 1946)

SERVES 8

For the marinade:

½ cup soy sauce

½ cup apricot jam or orange marmalade

¼–½ cup light brown sugar or honey

2 tablespoons rice vinegar

1 teaspoon crushed red pepper flakes

4½–5 pounds sirloin steak tips

1½ teaspoons kosher salt

½ teaspoon black pepper

2 scallions, chopped, for garnish

Place the marinade ingredients in a small bowl and mix well. Place the steak tips in a glass or ceramic bowl, or in a resealable plastic bag, and add the marinade. Cover or seal, and refrigerate at least 3 hours and up to overnight. Turn occasionally. (The steaks can be frozen up to 3 months.)

Preheat a grill or broiler.

Remove the steak and discard the marinade. Sprinkle the steak with the salt and pepper. Place the meat on a roasting pan or on a hot grill rack, and cook 4–5 minutes per side for medium-rare. Garnish with the scallions and serve immediately.

Flank Steak with Bourbon Balsamic Ginger

Flavors from the American South, Italy and Asia make this mellow marinade something special. Serve the steak with jasmine rice and steamed asparagus or broccoli.

SERVES 6

For the marinade:

¼ cup bourbon
¼ cup balsamic vinegar
3 tablespoons light brown sugar
2 tablespoons finely chopped gingerroot
½ teaspoon black pepper

2 flank steaks (2¾–3½ pounds)
1½ teaspoons kosher salt

TO PREPARE THE MARINADE: Place the marinade ingredients in a small bowl and mix well. Place the steaks in a glass or ceramic bowl, or in a resealable plastic bag, and add the marinade. Cover or seal, and refrigerate at least 3 hours and up to overnight. Turn occasionally. (The steaks can be frozen up to 3 months.)

Preheat a grill or broiler.

Remove the steaks and discard the marinade. Sprinkle the steaks with the salt. Place them on a roasting pan or on a hot grill rack, and cook 4–5 minutes per side for medium-rare.

Transfer the steaks to a cutting board and thinly slice against the grain. Serve immediately.

Shish Kebab

Grill some pitas or flatbread to serve alongside these succulent skewers.

SERVES 8–10

For the meat:

4½–5 pounds sirloin tips, cut into cubes

1 cup dry white wine

10–12 garlic cloves, chopped or pressed

1 red onion, chopped

2 tablespoons dried Greek oregano

For the sauce (optional):

4 garlic cloves, finely chopped or pressed

2 tablespoons red wine vinegar

2 cups full- or low-fat plain yogurt

1 teaspoon kosher salt

1 teaspoon black pepper

Fresh mint, for garnish

For the vegetables:

16–24 cherry tomatoes

16–24 button mushrooms

2 large red, orange or yellow bell peppers, cut into 16–24 pieces total

2 zucchini, cut into 16–24 cubes total

2 red onions, peeled keeping the root intact, cut into 8 wedges

TO PREPARE THE MEAT: Place the beef, wine, garlic, onion and oregano in a shallow glass or ceramic bowl, or in a resealable plastic bag. Cover or seal, and refrigerate overnight or freeze up to 3 months.

Preheat a grill or broiler. Place 24 skewers in a deep bowl of water and set aside to soak.

TO PREPARE THE SAUCE, IF USING: Place the garlic, vinegar, yogurt, salt and pepper in a small bowl and mix well. Cover and refrigerate. (The sauce can be made up to 2 days ahead.)

Remove the meat and discard as much of the marinade as possible. Remove the skewers from the water. Place the meat, tomatoes, mushrooms, bell peppers, zucchini and red onions on the skewers, filling each skewer with just one item (do not mix the meat and vegetables on the skewers). Place the skewers on the grill or under the broiler, and cook, turning every 1½ minutes, until the beef is deeply browned on the outside and rare in the inside, 8–10 minutes total.

Garnish with the fresh mint, and serve the sauce, if desired, on the side.

Rib Eye / Sirloin Steaks

Flavored Butters for Steak

Make these butters ahead of time and keep a couple of logs in the fridge or freezer to slice as needed. I like to keep a selection on hand and place coins of them on a plate so that my guests can choose. They're also good on chicken.

YIELD: EACH RECIPE, ABOUT ½ CUP FLAVORED BUTTER

Horseradish Butter

½ cup unsalted butter, at room temperature

2 tablespoons prepared horseradish

1 teaspoon kosher salt

2 tablespoons minced fresh chives (optional)

Cilantro Butter

½ cup unsalted butter, at room temperature
4 garlic cloves, minced
¼ cup finely chopped fresh cilantro leaves
2 teaspoons grated lime zest
½ teaspoon kosher salt
½ teaspoon crushed red pepper flakes

Anchovy Butter

½ cup unsalted butter, at room temperature
4 anchovy fillets, minced
2 tablespoons capers, drained
Grated zest and juice of 1 lemon

Chipotle Butter

½ cup unsalted butter, at room temperature
2 large chipotle chiles in adobo, finely chopped (page 184)
1 teaspoon adobo sauce
½ teaspoon kosher salt

Place the butter in a small bowl and mash until smooth. Add the remaining ingredients and mix until combined. Place on a large piece of waxed paper and form into a log. Cover with waxed paper and transfer to a resealable plastic bag. Use immediately, cover and refrigerate 2 weeks, or freeze up to 2 months. Slice into coin-size slices and serve over grilled or broiled steak.

Steak with Cumin and Chipotle

This crackly rub works equally well on pork, chicken and shrimp. Serve with warm tortillas instead of bread and your favorite salsa on the side.

> "Hospitality, n. The virtue which induces us to feed and lodge certain persons who are not in need of food and lodging."
> —AMBROSE BIERCE, JOURNALIST AND SHORT-STORY WRITER (1842–1914?)

SERVES 6–8

6 tablespoons light brown sugar

2–3 teaspoons chili powder or chipotle chile powder

1 tablespoon ground cumin

2 tablespoons kosher salt

4 sirloin or rib-eye steaks

Prepare a grill or preheat the broiler.

Place the brown sugar, chili powder, cumin and salt in a small bowl and mix well. Rub into the steaks.

Place the steaks 3–4 inches from the heat source and cook until slightly charred, 4–5 minutes per side for medium-rare. Transfer to a cutting board and let rest 5 minutes before slicing and serving.

Cowboy Steak au Poivre

My nephews, Michael and Nadav Nirenberg, both beg for this dish. In fact, they convinced me that Nadav needed a supply of the rub to bring to college: he makes this in his dorm room!

I serve this accompanied by a romaine salad dressed with blue cheese.

> "Too much of a good thing can be wonderful."
> —MAE WEST, ACTRESS (1893–1980)

SERVES 6–8

2 tablespoons kosher salt

2–3 tablespoons coarsely ground black pepper

¼ cup sugar

1 teaspoon cayenne pepper (optional)

4 sirloin or rib-eye steaks

Place the salt, black pepper, sugar and, if desired, the cayenne on a large plate and mix to combine. Dredge the steaks in the mixture. (You can prepare the steak up to 8 hours ahead: cover and refrigerate it, and then grill while it is still cold.)

Prepare a grill or preheat the broiler.

Place the steaks 3–4 inches from the heat source and cook until slightly charred, 4–5 minutes per side for medium-rare. Transfer to a cutting board and let rest for 5 minutes before slicing and serving.

Beef Stews and Braises

Nothing is more satisfying on a cold night than a stew or braised meat. And since these dishes are even better a day (or more) after they're cooked and freeze beautifully, I think of them as convenience foods.

I often find pre-cut stew meat chunks a little unwieldy; I prefer my ingredients in bite-size pieces and always cut the meat into smaller cubes. I think it makes the stew easier to eat, but this is really a matter of taste and doesn't affect the flavor of the dish.

Beef Carbonnade

I've been making this stew for twenty years, ever since pal Sharon Smith returned from Belgium with this recipe for beef and vegetables slowly simmered in beer. Even if you don't like the flavor of beer, try this; the alcohol and the bitterness cook out and leave behind a deep, rich sauce.

It is very important that you dry the meat well, or it will not brown properly.

If possible, make this the day before you want to serve it. Serve it with steamed new potatoes or boiled noodles.

> "Non-cooks think it's silly to invest two hours' work in two minutes' enjoyment; but if cooking is evanescent, well, so is the ballet."
> —JULIA CHILD, CHEF AND COOKBOOK AUTHOR (1912–2004)

YIELD: 12 CUPS; SERVES 6–8

½ pound bacon, chopped, *or* 1 tablespoon unsalted butter or olive oil

5 pounds beef stew meat, cut into 1–1½-inch cubes

2 teaspoons kosher salt

1 teaspoon black pepper

2 tablespoons unsalted butter

2 large Spanish onions, halved and sliced

1 teaspoon sugar

6 carrots, cut in large chunks

3 parsnips *or* 2 large potatoes, cut in large chunks

1 large turnip or 3–4 small turnips, cut in large chunks

3 celery stalks, cut in large chunks

2 teaspoons dried thyme

¼ cup all-purpose flour

Two 12-ounce bottles dark beer

1 cup beef broth

1 tablespoon Dijon mustard

1 teaspoon fresh thyme leaves, for garnish

½ cup fresh Italian flat-leaf parsley leaves, for garnish

Place a large Dutch oven over medium heat and when it is hot, add the bacon. Cook until rendered of fat and lightly browned, 8–10 minutes. Remove the bacon with a slotted spoon and place it on a large plate. Discard all but 1 tablespoon bacon fat.

Dry the beef cubes well with paper towels and sprinkle with the salt and pepper. Add the butter to the bacon fat and when it is hot, add a batch of the beef, enough to make a single layer in the pot, and cook until deeply browned, about 3 minutes on each side. Set the beef cubes aside and repeat until all the beef is browned; set aside.

Reheat the Dutch oven over medium heat, add the onions and sugar and cook until the onions have caramelized, about 30 minutes. Add the vegetables and thyme and cook, covered, for 10 minutes. Gradually add the flour, stirring constantly. Then gradually add the beer and beef broth. Add the reserved bacon and beef cubes and stir. Then cook, partially covered, over low heat until the beef is tender, about 2 hours. Stir in the mustard.

Serve immediately or transfer to a container, cover and refrigerate up to 2 days, or freeze up to 3 months. Just prior to serving, garnish with the fresh thyme and parsley.

Beef Chili

While I love to eat chili, I especially like to make it. I love the process—the way it makes my house smell and the way the windows fog up. I love that you can vary it endlessly and how the little changes make big differences.

I couldn't possibly count the number of variations I have made, but I think this may be the last because it is simply the best. It's a beefeater's chili, with a combination of cubed and ground beef that creates a unique texture. If you prefer, you can substitute ground pork or chicken for the ground beef. If you're a chili purist, don't add the tomatoes or beans. My preference is to add them.

YIELD: ABOUT 16 CUPS; SERVES 6–8

5 pounds beef stew meat, cut into 1–1½-inch cubes

2 teaspoons kosher salt

1 teaspoon black pepper

2 tablespoons olive oil

2 large Spanish onions, halved and chopped

2 red onions, halved and chopped

12–15 garlic cloves, chopped

2 pounds ground beef

6 tablespoons chili powder

2 tablespoons crushed red pepper flakes

2 teaspoons ground cumin

2 teaspoons ground cinnamon

2 teaspoons dried oregano

4 chipotle chiles in adobo, chopped

4 cups beer, beef broth, or Chicken Stock (page 8)

Four 16-ounce cans diced tomatoes (optional)

Four 16-ounce cans dark red kidney or black beans, drained and rinsed (optional)

½ cup chopped fresh cilantro leaves

Fresh lime slices

Sour cream (optional)

Grated cheddar cheese (optional)

Preheat the oven to 250 degrees.

Dry the beef cubes well with paper towels and sprinkle with the salt and pepper. Place a large ovenproof pot over medium-high heat and when it is hot, add the oil. Add a single layer of beef cubes and cook until deeply browned, about 3 minutes on each side. Set the beef cubes aside and repeat until all the beef is browned. Return the set-aside beef to the pot and add the onions and garlic. Cook, stirring occasionally and scraping up the browned bits, until the onions are softened, about 20 minutes.

Add the ground beef, spices, oregano and chipotles and cook until the beef loses its rawness, about 10 minutes. Add the beer, ½ cup at a time, allowing it to become slightly absorbed between additions. Transfer the pot to the oven and cook until the beef cubes are very tender, about 1½ hours. If desired, add the tomatoes and/or beans and cook for an additional ½ hour. Cover and refrigerate overnight or freeze up to 3 months.

Serve garnished with the cilantro and lime. Top with sour cream and/or cheddar cheese, if desired.

> "Wish I had time for just one more bowl of chili."
> —ALLEGED LAST WORDS OF KIT CARSON, FRONTIERSMAN (1809–1868)

Beef Bourguignon

The *Bourguignon* in Boeuf Bourguignon refers to Burgundy, the region of France where the dish originated. The original dish calls for tiny white onions but I have taken the liberty of substituting larger ones in order to reduce the amount of work: I don't think you lose any texture or flavor as a result.

I call for such a large quantity of bacon because no one in my family, myself included, has the self-control to wait for it to end up in the stew—we nibble on it while it's sitting on the plate. If you do have such self-control, start out with only ¼ pound. You can also leave the bacon out and substitute 1 tablespoon olive oil.

YIELD: ABOUT 12–14 CUPS; SERVES 6–8

½ pound bacon, diced

2½ pounds beef chuck, cut into 1-inch cubes

1 teaspoon kosher salt

½ teaspoon black pepper

4 carrots, sliced diagonally into 1-inch chunks

1 large Spanish onion, halved and thinly sliced

1 celery stalk, finely chopped

3–4 garlic cloves, chopped

1 teaspoon fresh thyme leaves

1 tablespoon tomato paste

¼ cup all-purpose flour

2 cups dry red wine, such as a Burgundy

2 cups beef broth or Chicken Stock (page 8)

½ cup cognac or brandy

2 tablespoons unsalted butter

½–1 pound button mushrooms, stems discarded, caps thickly sliced

2 tablespoons chopped fresh Italian flat-leaf parsley leaves (optional)

Kosher salt and black pepper to taste

Preheat the oven to 250 degrees.

Place a large ovenproof pot over medium heat and when it is hot, add the bacon. Cook until rendered of fat and lightly browned, 8–10 minutes. Remove the bacon with a slotted spoon and place it on a large plate. Discard all but 1 tablespoon bacon fat. Dry the beef cubes well with paper towels and sprinkle with the salt and pepper. Add the beef to the pot and cook until well browned, about 3 minutes per side. Set the beef aside on the same plate as the bacon.

Place the carrots, onion, celery, garlic and thyme in the hot pot and cook until lightly browned, about 10 minutes. Return the beef and bacon to the pot and stir well. Add the tomato paste. Add the flour, 1 tablespoon at a time, stirring all the while. When all the flour has been incorporated, add the wine and beef broth, 1 cup at a time. Bring just to a boil.

Cover the pot and transfer it to the oven. Cook until the meat is tender, about 2½ hours. Cover and refrigerate at least overnight and up to 2 days, or freeze up to 3 months.

To serve, add the cognac to the pot and stir well. Place over high heat and bring to a boil. Then lower the heat and cook, uncovered, until warmed throughout, 5–10 minutes.

While the stew is heating, place a medium-size saucepan over medium heat, add the butter, and when it has melted, add the mushrooms and cook until lightly browned, about 10 minutes. Add to the stew and cook for 5 minutes. Sprinkle with the parsley, season with salt and pepper, and serve.

> "If more of us valued food and cheer and song above hoarded gold, it would be a merrier world."
>
> —J.R.R. TOLKIEN, AUTHOR (1892–1973)

Irene Diller's Brisket
with Dried Fruit

Irene Diller is my friend Susan Benett's mother. About ten years ago I had a New Year's Day party and Susan offered to bring her mother's brisket. I wasn't a fan of brisket but accepted her offer. Susan's version of her mother's recipe included some Vietnamese chili garlic paste, which is not even remotely traditional. Even though I was sure I wouldn't like it, I tasted the brisket—and ate and ate and ate. I absolutely loved it. So even if this doesn't sound like something you'd like, try it: you'll like it.

SERVES 6–8

5½–6 pounds beef brisket

2 tablespoons kosher salt

1 tablespoon black pepper

1 tablespoon olive or vegetable oil

6 garlic cloves, chopped

3 large Spanish onions, halved and chopped

2 cups dry red wine

Two 6-ounce cans tomato paste

3–4 cups water

¼ cup light brown sugar

1 cup (about 20) pitted dried prunes, halved if desired

1 cup (about 30) dried apricots, halved if desired

1½ pounds carrots, cut in large chunks

3 medium russet or sweet potatoes, cut in large chunks (optional)

1–4 tablespoons Vietnamese chili garlic sauce (optional)

Kosher salt and black pepper to taste

Fresh or prepared horseradish, for serving

2 lemons, quartered, for serving

Preheat the oven to 325 degrees.

Pat the brisket dry with paper towels and season with the salt and pepper.

Place a large ovenproof pot over high heat and when it is hot, add the oil. Add the brisket and cook until seared, about 6 minutes on each side. Transfer to a plate and set aside.

Reheat the pot, add the garlic and onions and cook until soft and slightly golden, 10–15 minutes, stirring often. Add the red wine and cook for 2 minutes. Stir in 1 can tomato paste.

Add the brisket, fat side up. Spread the remaining tomato paste in a thick coating over the meat. Pour the water and brown sugar into the bottom of the pot. Do not pour it over the brisket. Bring the mixture to a boil, cover, transfer to the oven and cook for 1½ hours.

Add the prunes, apricots, carrots and, if desired, the potatoes. The vegetables should be submerged in the liquid; add more water if necessary. Cover the pot, return it to the oven, and continue cooking until the meat and vegetables are very tender, about 1 hour. Add the chili garlic paste, if desired.

Turn off the heat but let the pot sit in the oven for 30 minutes. Remove the brisket and let it cool until you can handle it, about ½ hour. Slice it thinly against the grain, and return it to the pot. Cover and refrigerate up to 2 days or freeze up to 3 months.

To serve, reheat the sliced brisket in the sauce on top of the stove. Add more salt and pepper, if necessary, and serve with horseradish and lemon quarters.

"Cooking is like love—it should be entered into with abandon or not at all."

—HARRIET VAN HORNE, JOURNALIST (1920–1998)

Pork and Lamb

Like most Americans, most of my meat eating is beef, but whenever I cook pork and lamb, I am so pleased I vow to eat more of them. I'll admit the price of lamb makes it right for a special dinner, but pork is less expensive and more versatile.

Brine for Pork

Once you've tasted a brined pork chop, you'll never go back. If you do nothing else when you buy pork, whether tenderloin or bone-in, follow this recipe and freeze the chops in portions. This way, you'll have succulent pork chops anytime.

> "The cure for anything is salt water—sweat, tears, or the sea."
> —ISAK DINESEN, WRITER (1885–1962)

¾ cup kosher salt
¾ cup light brown sugar
1 cup boiling water
9–12 boneless pork chops
7 cups cold water

Place the salt, sugar and boiling water in a small bowl and mix until the salt and sugar are dissolved.

Place the pork in a gallon-size resealable plastic bag or other large container. Cover with the cold water and then add the saltwater mixture. Cover or seal, and refrigerate at least 1 hour and up to 8.

Remove the pork chops from the brine and rinse them well with cold water. Place them in the refrigerator, uncovered, for at least 1 hour and up to 8 hours to air-dry.

Use immediately, cover and refrigerate up to 2 days, or freeze up to 1 month. Use in your favorite recipe for pork chops.

Dijon Pork Chops

This classic combination of pork, mustard and apple is perfect for a quick weekday dinner. Serve the chops with applesauce, baked sweet potatoes and a green salad.

> "He who distinguishes the true savor of his food can never be a glutton; he who does not cannot be otherwise."
> —HENRY DAVID THOREAU, WRITER, NATURALIST (1817–1862)

SERVES 4–5

1–2 tablespoons unsalted butter, or olive or canola oil
4–5 boneless pork chops (about 3 pounds)
1½ teaspoons kosher salt
½ teaspoon black pepper
⅓ cup Dijon mustard
1 cup apple juice or cider

Place a large skillet over medium-high heat and when it is hot, add the butter. Sprinkle the pork chops with the salt and pepper and place in the skillet. Cook until lightly browned, 4–7 minutes on each side, depending on the thickness.

Transfer the chops to a platter, and add the mustard and apple juice to the pan. Bring to a boil and pour over the chops. Serve immediately.

Sautéed Pork Chops with Vinegar and Bell Peppers

A delicious and very traditional Italian dish with slightly sweet and sour flavors.

SERVES 4

4 bone-in 12-ounce thick-cut pork chops
½ teaspoon kosher salt
½ teaspoon black pepper
2 tablespoons olive oil

For the peppers:

2 garlic cloves, minced
2 anchovy fillets, minced
1 red bell pepper, diced
1 yellow bell pepper, diced
1 rosemary branch, 4–5 inches long, or 1 marjoram sprig,
    6 inches long
1 cup water
½ cup white wine vinegar

Preheat the oven to 450 degrees. Place a shallow roasting pan in the oven.

Sprinkle the chops with the salt and pepper. Place a 12-inch heavy-bottomed ovenproof skillet over high heat and when it is hot, add the oil. Add the chops and cook until well browned and crusted, about 3 minutes on each side. Transfer the skillet to the oven and cook for about 4 minutes on each side (until the chops register about 145 degrees). Turn off the heat. Transfer the chops to the roasting pan in the oven.

TO PREPARE THE PEPPERS: Reheat the skillet. Add the garlic, anchovies, bell peppers and rosemary and cook until the peppers are soft, 4–5 minutes. Add ½ cup water and the vinegar and bring to a boil, stirring and scraping up any browned bits. Cook until the liquid has almost evaporated, about 6 minutes. Add the remaining ½ cup water and cook until the mixture is syrupy, 3–4 minutes. Discard the rosemary. Return the chops to the skillet.

Spoon the peppers over the chops and serve immediately from the skillet.

Pork Chops with Apricot Mustard Sauce

A more sophisticated version of Dijon Pork Chops (page 219), but without much more work. Serve these with a watercress salad and mashed potatoes.

> "There are no secrets to success. It is the result of preparation, hard work, and learning from failure."
>
> —COLIN POWELL, GENERAL AND STATESMAN (B. 1937)

SERVES 4

1 teaspoon olive oil
4 boneless pork chops (about 1¾–2 pounds)
1 teaspoon kosher salt
½–1 teaspoon black pepper
2 tablespoons apricot or peach preserves
3 heaping tablespoons Dijon mustard
2 teaspoons light brown sugar
1 tablespoon balsamic vinegar

Place a large skillet over medium-high heat and when it is hot, add the oil. Sprinkle the chops with the salt and pepper and place in the skillet. Cook until well browned, 4–7 minutes on each side. Add the preserves, mustard and brown sugar and stir until the chops are well coated. Transfer the chops to a platter.

Raise the heat to high and add the balsamic vinegar. Bring to a boil, stirring well. Pour the mixture over the chops and serve immediately.

Pork Chops with Rosemary, Garlic and Fennel

Peppery and sweet, these are perfect for a cold fall or winter day. Serve them with roasted squash or sweet potatoes and steamed rice.

SERVES 4

1 teaspoon kosher salt
½ teaspoon black pepper
½ teaspoon coarsely ground fennel seed
1 teaspoon fresh rosemary leaves, coarsely chopped
4 boneless pork chops (about 1¾–2 pounds)
3 teaspoons olive or canola oil
2 garlic cloves, minced
½–⅔ cup fresh orange juice
1 tablespoon apricot or peach jam

Place the salt, pepper, fennel and rosemary on a plate and mix to combine. Dredge the pork chops in the mixture, pressing the mixture into them.

Place a large skillet over medium-high heat and when it is hot, add 2 teaspoons oil. Add the pork chops and cook until well browned, 4–5 minutes on each side. Transfer the chops to a plate and cover with aluminum foil. Lower the heat to low, add the remaining 1 teaspoon oil, and when it is hot, add the garlic. When the garlic is just golden, add the juice and jam. Bring to a boil and cook, stirring, for 2 minutes. Return the chops to the skillet and cook for 1 minute. Serve immediately.

Orange-Marinated Pork

Sweet, salty and tangy, this dish can be served with rice and any sautéed green, such as broccoli rabe or kale.

SERVES 4–6

> "As a child my family's menu consisted of two choices: take it or leave it."
>
> —BUDDY HACKETT, COMEDIAN (1924–2003)

4–6 boneless pork chops
¾ cup orange juice
2 tablespoons soy sauce
2 tablespoons light brown sugar
2 teaspoons minced fresh gingerroot
Juice and grated zest of 1 lime
1 ripe peach, nectarine or mango, diced
1 teaspoon kosher salt
½ teaspoon black pepper

Place everything, except the fruit, salt and pepper, in a shallow bowl or pan, and stir to mix. Cover and refrigerate at least 20 minutes and up to 4 hours.

Prepare a grill.

Place the pork chops on the grill, sprinkle with salt and pepper and cook for about 5 minutes per side, basting all the while with the liquid from the marinade. Serve immediately, topped with the fruit.

Latin Pork Chops

Serve these spicy chops with braised greens, any kind of roasted root vegetable, and/or steamed rice. The marinade can also be used on chicken, steak or lamb chops, either as a marinade or as a sauce after the meat has been cooked.

SERVES 4–6

4–6 boneless pork chops

Juice and grated zest of 1 lime

4 garlic cloves, minced

1 tablespoon chili powder or chipotle chile powder, or a combination

1 teaspoon ground cumin

2 tablespoons olive oil

2 tablespoons orange juice

2–3 tablespoons finely chopped fresh cilantro leaves

1 teaspoon kosher salt

½ teaspoon black pepper

Place everything, except the salt and pepper, in a glass or ceramic bowl, and mix well. Cover and refrigerate at least 1 hour and up to 4.

Preheat a grill to very hot.

Sprinkle the pork chops with the salt and pepper and place them on the grill. Cook until faintly pink in the inside and crusted on the outside, about 5 minutes on each side. Serve immediately. (Pork is completely cooked at 137–140 degrees, which is the way I like it. If you prefer yours more well done, simply increase the cooking time.)

Chili-Coated Pork Chops

Spicy but not too hot, these Southwestern-flavored chops make a great fast weeknight dinner. Try them with Spanish rice and corn.

> "I told my doctor I get very tired when I go on a diet, so he gave me pep pills. Know what happened? I ate faster."
> —JOE E. LEWIS, COMEDIAN AND SINGER (1902–1971)

SERVES 4

1 teaspoon chili powder

1 teaspoon ground cumin

1 teaspoon kosher salt

½ teaspoon black pepper

4 boneless pork chops (about 1¾–2 pounds)

1 tablespoon olive oil

2–3 garlic cloves, minced

Juice and grated zest of 1 lime

3 tablespoons finely chopped fresh cilantro leaves

1 lime, quartered, for garnish

Preheat the oven to 400 degrees.

Place the chili powder, cumin, salt and pepper in a small bowl and mix well. Rub the mixture on both sides of the pork chops.

Place a large ovenproof skillet over high heat and when it is hot, add the oil. Add the pork chops, waiting about 30 seconds between additions, and cook until seared, about 1 minute on each side. Add the garlic, lime juice and zest and cilantro and transfer the skillet to the oven. Roast until the chops are faintly pink on the inside and crusted on the outside, about 10 minutes. (Pork is completely cooked at 137–140 degrees, which is the way I like it. If you prefer yours more well done, simply increase the cooking time.) Serve immediately, garnished with the lime quarters.

Honey Dijon Baby Back Ribs

Sticky and delicious.

> "In the course of my life, I have often had to eat my words, and I must confess that I have always found it a wholesome diet."
> — WINSTON CHURCHILL, STATESMAN (1874–1965)

SERVES 6–8

⅔ cup Dijon mustard

⅔ cup honey

2 tablespoons toasted sesame oil

2 tablespoons soy sauce

½ cup red or white wine vinegar

½ cup light brown sugar

3 slabs baby back ribs (6–7 pounds), each slab cut in half

1 teaspoon kosher salt

½ teaspoon black pepper

Place the mustard, honey, sesame oil, soy sauce, vinegar and brown sugar in a small bowl and mix well. Place the ribs in a large glass or ceramic bowl, or in a resealable plastic bag, add the mustard mixture and mix well. Cover or seal, and refrigerate at least overnight and up to 2 days. Turn occasionally. (The ribs can be frozen up to 3 months.)

Preheat the oven to 300 degrees.

Discard the marinade and place the ribs, meat side up, in a large baking pan. Sprinkle with the salt and pepper and cook for 3–4 hours, or until cooked throughout, brown and crusty.

Drain off any fat and serve immediately.

Asian Ribs

Serve this with jasmine rice and steamed or sautéed snow peas.

SERVES 6–8

⅓ cup light molasses
⅓ cup sake
¼ cup soy sauce
¼ cup apple cider vinegar
3 tablespoons chopped fresh gingerroot
4 garlic cloves, minced
2 teaspoons five-spice powder
3 slabs baby back ribs (6–7 pounds), each slab cut in half
1 teaspoon kosher salt
½ teaspoon black pepper
4 scallions, chopped. for garnish

Place the molasses, sake, soy sauce, vinegar, ginger, garlic and five-spice powder in a small bowl and mix well. Place the ribs in a large glass or ceramic bowl, or in a re-sealable plastic bag, add the molasses mixture and mix well. Cover or seal, and refrigerate at least overnight and up to 2 days. Turn occasionally. (The ribs can be frozen up to 3 months.)

Preheat the oven to 300 degrees.

Discard the marinade and place the ribs, meat side up, in a large baking pan. Sprinkle with the salt and pepper and cook for 3–4 hours, or until cooked throughout, brown and crusty.

Drain off any fat and serve immediately, garnished with the scallions.

Laurie Colwin's Crisp, Sweet Ribs

These ribs are inspired by the recipe in Laurie Colwin's book, *Home Cooking.* She describes them as "crisp and tender, salty, sweet, oily but not greasy and very garlicky." I agree.

SERVES 6–8

1 cup soy sauce
½ cup olive oil
½ cup honey or brown sugar
Grated zest and juice of 1 lemon
8 garlic cloves, minced
3 slabs baby back ribs (6–7 pounds), each slab cut in half
1 teaspoon kosher salt
½ teaspoon black pepper
4 scallions, chopped, for garnish

Place the soy sauce, olive oil, honey, lemon zest and juice and garlic in a small bowl and mix well. Place the ribs in a large glass or ceramic bowl, or in a resealable plastic bag, add the soy mixture and mix well. Cover or seal, and refrigerate at least overnight and up to 2 days. Turn occasionally. (The ribs can be frozen up to 3 months.)

Preheat the oven to 300 degrees.

Discard the marinade and place the ribs, meat side up, in a large baking pan. Sprinkle with the salt and pepper and cook for 3–4 hours, or until cooked throughout and brown and crusty.

Drain off any fat and serve immediately, garnished with the scallions.

Parmesan-Crusted Lamb Chops

I never liked lamb chops until I made this Italian-inspired recipe. I use the classic breading technique of dusting (with cheese instead of flour), dipping (in egg) and coating (with bread crumbs), which makes these chops delicate and special enough for a dinner party.

SERVES 4–6

½–1 cup finely grated Parmesan cheese

2 large eggs, beaten

1½–2 cups fine Fresh Bread Crumbs (page 11)

1 teaspoon finely chopped fresh rosemary leaves

2 teaspoons finely chopped fresh mint leaves

12–16 lamb rib chops (2¾–3 pounds), cut ¾–1 inch thick

½ teaspoon kosher salt

¼ teaspoon black pepper

¼ cup olive oil

1 lemon, cut into 8 wedges, for garnish

Place the Parmesan cheese on a plate. Place the eggs in a shallow bowl. Place the bread crumbs, rosemary and mint on a plate and mix to combine.

Sprinkle the chops with the salt and pepper.

Dip the chops, one at a time, in the Parmesan, patting it down to make sure the cheese adheres. Dip the chops in the eggs and then in the bread crumb mixture, patting it down and then shaking off any excess. Transfer the breaded chops to a wire rack placed over a plate. Refrigerate, uncovered, at least ½ hour and up to 4 hours.

Place a large skillet over medium-high heat and when it is hot, add the oil (the oil should reach halfway up the sides of the chops). Add half the chops, one at a time, allowing the pan to reheat for 30 seconds before each addition, and cook until well browned on the outside and rare on the inside (the meat should register about 135–140 degrees), 2–3 minutes on each side. Drain on a paper towel.

Reheat the oil and repeat with the remaining chops. Transfer the chops to a heated serving platter and serve immediately, garnished with the lemon wedges.

Fish and Seafood

The ultimate fast food, fish takes minutes to cook. Like chicken, most types of fish are infinitely flexible and take well to a variety of seasonings.

Tuna and Salmon

Broiled Salmon with Mustard and Brown Sugar

Making dinner doesn't get any simpler than this. Slathered in a slightly sweet, spicy mustard sauce, this salmon is great paired with a dark green vegetable. I'm partial to broccoli myself.

> "You don't get over hating to cook, any more than you get over having big feet." — PEG BRACKEN, HUMORIST (B. 1918)

SERVES 6

1½–2 pounds salmon fillet, tiny bones removed with a tweezer, cut in half

2 tablespoons Dijon mustard

2 tablespoons light brown sugar

½ teaspoon chili powder

½ teaspoon kosher salt

Preheat the broiler.

Place the mustard, brown sugar and chili powder in a small bowl and mix to combine.

Place the salmon in a large baking dish and smother with the mustard mixture.

(The salmon can be covered and refrigerated up to 4 hours or frozen up to 2 weeks.) Sprinkle with the salt and place under the broiler. Cook until browned on top and just undercooked inside, 5–6 minutes.

Cut each half into 3 pieces and serve immediately.

Chili-Crusted Salmon

Perfect served with white rice and a big green salad. You can substitute swordfish steaks for the salmon.

> "Give a man a fish and you feed him for a day. Teach a man to fish and you feed him for a lifetime."   —PROVERB

SERVES 6

3 tablespoons chili powder

1 tablespoon ground cumin

2 teaspoons dried basil

1 teaspoon kosher salt

1 tablespoon olive oil

2 pounds salmon fillet, tiny bones removed with a tweezer, cut in half

1 lemon, cut into 6 wedges

Place the chili powder, cumin, basil and salt on a large plate, and mix well. Dredge the salmon in the mixture.

Place a large skillet over medium-high heat and when it is hot, add the oil.

Add the salmon, skin side down first, and cook until browned and firm, 3–4 minutes per side. Cut each half into 3 pieces. Serve immediately, with the lemon wedges.

Grilled Salmon with Sesame Citrus Vinaigrette

This is the salmon recipe with the longest list of ingredients, but most cooks will have the majority of them on hand. It is a very special and unforgettable dish.

Serve this with rice and a watercress or spinach salad.

> "A man hath no better thing under the sun, than to eat, and to drink, and to be merry."
>
> —ECCLESIASTES 8:15

SERVES 6

For the vinaigrette:

2 tablespoons olive oil
1 garlic clove, minced
1 teaspoon finely chopped fresh gingerroot
½ cup chopped red onion
2 tablespoons sesame seeds
¼ cup fresh lemon or lime juice
¼ cup orange, apple or pineapple juice
¼ teaspoon sugar
1 tablespoon balsamic vinegar
1 tablespoon finely chopped fresh basil or cilantro leaves
2 scallion greens, finely chopped
¼–½ teaspoon kosher salt
¼–½ teaspoon black pepper

2 pounds salmon fillet, tiny bones removed with a tweezer, cut in half
1 teaspoon kosher salt
½ teaspoon black pepper
1 tablespoon olive oil

Prepare a grill.

TO MAKE THE VINAIGRETTE: Place a large skillet over medium heat and when it is hot, add the 2 tablespoons of oil. Add the garlic, ginger, onion and sesame seeds and cook until the vegetables are soft and the seeds are lightly browned, about 5 minutes. Off heat, add the juices, sugar, vinegar, basil, scallion greens, salt and pepper. (The vinaigrette can be covered and refrigerated up to 4 hours.)

Brush 1 tablespoon oil over the salmon and sprinkle with the salt and pepper. Place the salmon on the grill and cook for 3–4 minutes per side. Transfer the salmon to a serving platter and top with the vinaigrette. Serve immediately.

Brown Butter—Roasted Salmon with Mint

The richness of brown (not burnt!) butter and the fresh taste of mint make this dish elegant enough for a dinner party, simple enough for everyday.

SERVES 6

2 pounds salmon fillet, tiny bones removed with a tweezer, cut in half

1 teaspoon kosher salt

½ teaspoon black pepper

1 tablespoon unsalted butter

¼ cup chopped fresh mint leaves, for garnish

1 lemon or lime, cut into 6 wedges, for garnish

Sprinkle the salmon with the salt and pepper.

Place a large skillet over medium-high heat and when it is hot, add the butter. Cook until the butter just starts to brown, 1–2 minutes Do not let the butter burn; if it does, pour it out, wipe out the pan and start again.

Add the salmon, skin side down first, and cook until it is browned and firm, 3–4 minutes per side. Serve immediately, garnished with the mint and the lemon wedges.

Salmon on a Bed of Leeks and Carrots

As a fan of deeply browned food, this was another recipe I originally didn't think I'd like but totally love; it is light, easy and delicious.

> "The secret of staying young is to live honestly, eat slowly, and lie about your age."
>
> —LUCILLE BALL, ACTRESS (1911–1989)

SERVES 6

3 large leeks
2 teaspoons olive oil
3 carrots, julienned
1 teaspoon kosher salt, or more to taste
½ teaspoon white pepper, or more to taste
¼ cup dry white vermouth or dry white wine
2 pounds salmon fillet, tiny bones removed with a tweezer, cut in half

Trim the roots off the leeks and remove all but 2 inches of the green part. Cut the leeks into very thin strips and wash them in several changes of hot water, being sure to get rid of any sand. Drain well in a colander.

Place a large skillet over medium heat and when it is hot, add the oil. Add the leeks and carrots and cook, stirring occasionally, until the carrots are just tender, 10 minutes.

Add the salt, pepper, vermouth and salmon, cover and cook for 10–12 minutes. Cut each piece of salmon into thirds and serve immediately.

Spicy Salsa Salmon Cakes

When you want the ease of a burger but are in the mood for fish, this is the perfect solution.

SERVES 4

1½ pounds salmon fillet, finely chopped

½ bunch scallions, chopped

1 large egg, lightly beaten

2 tablespoons mayonnaise

2 tablespoons Dijon mustard

½ cup salsa, plus additional for garnish

3–4 tablespoons chopped fresh cilantro leaves

¼ cup stone-ground yellow cornmeal

1 teaspoon kosher salt

2–3 tablespoons all-purpose flour

2 tablespoons olive oil

1 lime, quartered, for garnish

Place the salmon, scallions, egg, mayonnaise, mustard, salsa and cilantro in a large bowl and toss gently to combine.

Place the cornmeal, salt and flour on a large plate and stir to mix. Divide the salmon mixture into 4 portions and shape them into patties. Dredge them in the cornmeal mixture. Cover and refrigerate for at least ½ hour and up to 8 hours. (Freeze in a resealable plastic bag for up to 2 weeks.)

Place a large skillet over medium-high heat and when it is hot, add the oil. Add the patties and cook until well browned, about 3 minutes on each side.

Serve immediately, garnished with the lime quarters and additional salsa.

Tuna with Soy and Lime

Slightly Asian in flavor, this goes nicely with steamed rice and spinach.

> "If you're too busy to go fishin', you're too busy."
>
> —JED CLAMPETT, FROM *THE BEVERLY HILLBILLIES*

SERVES 4

4 tuna steaks, 6–8 ounces each
6 tablespoons soy sauce
3 teaspoons olive or canola oil
1 teaspoon toasted sesame oil
1 teaspoon fresh lime juice
Wasabi, for garnish (optional)
4 lime slices, for garnish

Place the tuna, soy sauce, 2 teaspoons olive oil, sesame oil and lime juice in a glass or ceramic dish, or in a resealable plastic bag, cover or seal, and refrigerate at least 30 minutes and up to 2 hours.

Remove as much of the marinade as possible. Place a skillet over high heat and when it is very hot, add the remaining 1 teaspoon olive oil. Add the tuna and cook about 2 minutes on each side. Serve immediately, garnished with the wasabi, if desired, and the lime slices.

Tuna au Poivre

A cross between steak au poivre and the classic Sicilian sauce *salmoriglio*, this dish is heady with the flavors of pepper, lemon and oregano.

If you want to freeze this, add the olive oil to the lemon/pepper mixture before dredging the tuna in it. Transfer the tuna to a plastic freezer bag and freeze. After you thaw it, cook the tuna in a dry pan; the olive oil in the marinade should be enough.

SERVES 4

1 tablespoon finely grated lemon zest
3–4 teaspoons coarsely ground black pepper
2 garlic cloves, finely minced
2 teaspoons dried oregano
1 teaspoon kosher salt
2 pounds tuna steaks, cut into 4 pieces
2 teaspoons olive oil
1 lemon, quartered

Place the lemon zest, pepper, garlic, oregano and salt on a large plate and mix to combine. Dredge the tuna in the mixture.

Place a large cast-iron skillet over medium-high heat and when it is hot, add the oil. Add the tuna and cook until browned, about 5 minutes on each side.

Serve immediately, garnished with the lemon quarters.

Tuna with Lime, Capers and Garlic

The meatiness of tuna stands up well to the strong flavors of lime, capers and garlic. While this dish needs to marinate for a while, it cooks up quickly.

> "Life is what happens when you are busy making other plans."
> —JOHN LENNON, MUSICIAN (1940–1980)

SERVES 4

4 tuna steaks, 6–8 ounces each
¼ cup olive oil
¼ cup dry white wine
1 teaspoon grated lime zest
1 garlic clove, minced
1 tablespoon capers, drained
1 shallot
1 teaspoon kosher salt
½ teaspoon black pepper
1 lime, quartered

Place the tuna in a glass or ceramic bowl.

Place the olive oil, wine, lime zest, garlic, capers and shallot in a food processor fitted with a steel blade and blend until smooth. Pour the marinade over the tuna, cover, and refrigerate for up to 4 hours, turning occasionally. (You can freeze the tuna for 2 weeks.)

Prepare a grill.

Sprinkle the tuna with the salt and pepper and place it on the grill. Cook, brushing it with the marinade, until lightly charred on the outside and rare in the inside. Serve immediately, with the lime quarters.

Blackened Tuna

With almost all the ingredients on hand, dinner doesn't get any easier than this. Serve the fish with a mesclun salad containing chunks of avocado and pineapple.

If you want to freeze this, add the olive oil to the spice rub before rubbing the tuna with it. Transfer the tuna to a plastic freezer bag and freeze. After you thaw the tuna, cook it in a dry pan; the olive oil in the marinade should be enough.

> "A person who is nice to you, but rude to the waiter, is not a nice person."
>
> —DAVE BARRY, WRITER AND HUMORIST (B. 1947)

SERVES 4

For the spice rub:

2 teaspoons dried Greek oregano

1 teaspoon cayenne pepper

2 teaspoons garlic powder

1 teaspoon dried thyme

1 teaspoon Hungarian paprika

1 teaspoon kosher salt

½ teaspoon black pepper

4 tuna or catfish fillets, 6–8 ounces each

2 teaspoons olive oil

1 lemon or lime, cut into 4 slices, for garnish

TO MAKE THE SPICE RUB: Place all the ingredients in a small bowl and combine well.

Place the tuna on a large plate and rub both sides with the spice mixture. (You can proceed immediately, or cover and refrigerate up to overnight.)

Prepare a grill or place a large skillet over high heat.

If you are grilling, lightly rub each side of the fish with the olive oil and cook the fish for 4–5 minutes on each side.

If you are pan-grilling, when the skillet is hot, add the oil. Add the fish and cook until deeply browned and cooked throughout, 4–5 minutes on each side.

Serve immediately, garnished with the lemon slices.

Shrimp and Scallops

I'd been shopping at price clubs for years before I discovered big bags of frozen raw shrimp and scallops. If you're a fan, it should be an indispensible item in your freezer, valued for simplicity, ease and flexibility.

Chili-Rubbed Shrimp

The first time I made this, I used jumbo shrimp and made six for myself. And then I made two more, and then another two. The next day, my friend David Zebny came over and I prepared more for lunch. The same thing happened: we just kept eating and eating. Suffice it to say, these are really addictive. This rub is also great on scallops and tuna. If you are using scallops, cook about 1 minute per side. If you are using tuna steaks, cook 2 minutes on the top and bottom and then 1 minute on each side.

As a rule, I am not fond of garlic powder and almost always prefer to use fresh garlic. However, I keep some on hand just to make this dish, where fresh garlic doesn't work as well.

> "There is no love sincerer than the love of food."
> —GEORGE BERNARD SHAW, PLAYWRIGHT (1856–1950)

SERVES 4–6

For the rub:

2 tablespoons chili powder

2 teaspoons garlic powder

2 teaspoons ground cumin

I teaspoon cayenne pepper

I teaspoon dried basil

I teaspoon dried marjoram

I teaspoon black pepper

I tablespoon kosher salt

I tablespoon olive oil

I tablespoon unsalted butter

2 pounds jumbo or large shrimp, peeled and deveined, dried with a paper towel

1–2 limes, quartered, for garnish

TO MAKE THE RUB: Place all the ingredients on a large plate and mix until well combined.

Place a large skillet over medium-high heat and when it is hot, add the oil and butter.

Dredge the shrimp in the rub. Place them in the skillet without crowding, 6–8 at a time, and sear until the edges become solid and curl, about 2 minutes per side. Serve immediately or at room temperature, garnished with the lime quarters.

Curried Shrimp

I keep a bag of uncooked shrimp in my freezer so that I can make a dish like this one with very little effort. Since I usually have everything else on hand, I only need to shop for the cilantro and pineapple.

Rich, creamy and slightly sweet, COCONUT MILK is made by cooking water and finely shredded coconut together and then straining it to remove all the pulp. The best brands have a thick cream that has risen to the top. Leftover coconut milk can be frozen in ice cube trays and then transferred to a resealable plastic bag.

SERVES 4–6

1 tablespoon olive oil
1 Spanish onion, halved and chopped
3 garlic cloves, minced
1 walnut-size chunk fresh gingerroot, minced
1–2 tablespoons curry powder
2 pounds shrimp, peeled and deveined
1 beefsteak tomato, chopped
½ cup coconut milk
½ cup Chicken Stock (page 8)
½ teaspoon cayenne pepper (optional)
½ teaspoon kosher salt
2–4 tablespoons chopped fresh cilantro leaves,
     plus additional for garnish
Cooked rice or noodles, for serving
1 cup chopped fresh pineapple, for garnish
1 cup chopped roasted cashews, for garnish

Place a skillet over medium heat and when it is hot, add the oil. Add the onion, garlic and ginger and cook until soft and light golden, about 5 minutes. Add the curry powder and cook for 1 minute.

Add the shrimp and cook for 2 minutes, stirring all the while. Add the tomato, coconut milk and chicken stock, lower the heat to low and cook for 5 minutes.

Add the cayenne, if desired, salt and cilantro and cook until heated through, about 1 minute. Serve immediately, on top of rice or noodles, garnished with the pineapple, cashews and extra cilantro.

Shrimp with Lime and Basil

Simple and flavorful. You can certainly use fewer shrimp per person, but I wouldn't.

SERVES 4–6

1 tablespoon olive oil

2 pounds large shrimp, peeled and deveined, well dried

1¼ teaspoons kosher salt

½ teaspoon black pepper

Juice and grated zest of 1 lime

¼ cup finely chopped fresh basil leaves

¼ teaspoon Vietnamese chili garlic sauce (optional)

Place a large skillet over medium-high heat and when it is hot, add the oil. Sprinkle the shrimp with the salt and pepper, place them in the skillet and cook until lightly browned, 2–3 minutes per side. Add the remaining ingredients and toss to combine. Serve immediately.

Scallops in Basil Oil

> "Govern a great nation as you would cook a small fish. Do not overdo it."
>
> — LAO TZU, TAOIST PHILOSOPHER (B. 600 BC)

SERVES 4–6

Juice of 1 lemon

¼ cup finely chopped fresh basil leaves

2 tablespoons olive oil

2 garlic cloves, minced

2 pounds sea scallops

1 teaspoon kosher salt

½ teaspoon black pepper

2 tablespoons unsalted butter

Place the lemon juice, basil, olive oil and garlic in a large bowl and mix well. Add the scallops and mix again. Cover and refrigerate at least ½ hour but no more than 1 hour.

Remove and discard as much of the marinade as possible from the scallops. Pat them dry with a paper towel. Sprinkle with the salt and pepper.

Place a large cast-iron skillet over high heat. When the skillet is hot, add the butter. When the butter has melted, add the scallops, a few at a time, allowing the pan to reheat for about 30 seconds between additions. Cook until seared and deeply browned, about 2 minutes per side. You will probably need to cook them in two batches.

Serve immediately.

Scallops in Caper Brown Butter

Though this tastes as if you had put in a lot of effort, it is amazingly speedy to make. With a bag of scallops in the freezer, you can have a company-worthy meal on the table in minutes.

> "I have the simplest tastes. I am always satisfied with the best."
> —OSCAR WILDE, DRAMATIST, NOVELIST AND POET (1854–1900)

SERVES 4–6

2 pounds scallops
1 teaspoon kosher salt
½ teaspoon black pepper
3 tablespoons unsalted butter
¼ cup capers, drained
1 lemon, cut in 4–6 wedges, for garnish

Pat the scallops dry with a paper towel. Sprinkle with the salt and pepper.

Place a large cast-iron skillet over high heat. When the skillet is hot, add 1 tablespoon butter. Add the scallops, a few at a time, allowing the pan to reheat for about 30 seconds between additions. Do not stir them but instead allow them to sear until deeply brown, about 2 minutes per side. You will probably need to cook them in two batches.

Transfer the cooked scallops to a plate and reheat the skillet. Add the capers and the remaining 2 tablespoons butter and cook until the butter just starts to brown, 1–2 minutes. Pour the mixture over the scallops and serve immediately, garnished with the lemon wedges.

Cocktail Pitchers

Alcoholic and Not

If you're having a party, or even just more than a few people over, and you don't want to end up mixing drinks all night, having a few recipes for Cocktail Pitchers can save the day. From Lemonade With and Without Rum (page 254) to Bloody Marys (page 256), there are alcoholic and nonalcoholic drinks here for all.

Mojito

Best described as sparkling mint limeade with rum, this classic Cuban cocktail is open to interpretation. My version has more lime and mint than the standard fare. It's a flavor combination I particularly love *and* since I have an endless supply of mint growing by the side of my house, it's an easy drink for me to whip up.

For a non-alcoholic mojito, simply omit the rum.

SERVES 6

For the simple syrup:

⅓ cup sugar
½ cup boiling water
1 bunch fresh mint sprigs
3 limes, thinly sliced or cut into wedges
6 ounces fresh lime juice (12 tablespoons or juice of 6 limes)
9 ounces light rum

Ice cubes
Seltzer

TO MAKE THE SIMPLE SYRUP: Place the sugar and water in a small heatproof glass and stir until the sugar has dissolved and the liquid is clear. Set aside to cool.

Place the mint leaves and lime slices in a large pitcher and muddle (slightly mash with the straight end of a wooden spoon) together.

Add the lime juice, cooled simple syrup and rum and mix well.

Fill six tall glasses with ice cubes and divide the mixture evenly between the glasses. Fill to the top with seltzer or club soda.

Lemonade With and Without Rum

There's nothing more refreshing on a hot day than fresh homemade lemonade. For a more adult version, add some rum. Although lemonade is delicious straight up, try it mixed half and half with either unsweetened iced tea or cranberry juice, for something delightfully different.

> "When fate hands you a lemon, make lemonade."
> —DALE CARNEGIE, LECTURER AND WRITER (1888–1955)

YIELD: 12 CUPS

1 cup sugar

2 cups boiling water

6 cups cold water

3 cups fresh lemon juice (about 12 lemons)

4 lemons, thinly sliced, for garnish

Fresh mint sprigs, for garnish (optional)

Place the sugar and boiling water in a heatproof pitcher and stir until the sugar has dissolved. Set aside to cool to room temperature. Cover and refrigerate overnight.

Add the cold water and lemon juice and serve immediately, garnished with sliced lemons and mint sprigs, if desired.

With rum:

FOR EACH 4-OUNCE GLASS OF LEMONADE, ADD:

½ lemon, cut in half

Sugar

Ice cubes

2½ tablespoons Myer's Original Dark Rum

½ tablespoon Rose's Lime Juice

Rub the rim of each glass with the cut end of the lemon half, and then turn the glass upside down onto a plate of sugar, coating the rim with the sugar. Fill the glass with ice cubes, and add the lemonade, rum and lime juice.

Nancita's Margarita

YIELD: 5½–6 CUPS

2½ cups limeade (made from concentrate, using 3 parts water
  instead of the recommended 4)
2 cups tequila
⅔ cup Triple Sec
½ cup fresh lime juice
2 limes, each cut into 10 pieces
Kosher salt
Ice cubes

Place the limeade, tequila, Triple Sec and lime juice in a large pitcher and mix well. Cover and refrigerate at least ½ hour and up to 4 hours.

Rub the rim of a margarita glass with a lime piece and then turn the glass upside down onto a plate of kosher salt, coating the rim with salt. Fill the glass with ice cubes and add the margarita mixture. Serve immediately, garnished with lime pieces.

Bloody Mary/Virgin Mary

Bloody or Virgin, this spicy, tangy drink is the classic accompaniment to a lazy Sunday brunch. It also delivers substantial amounts of vitamin C and other important nutrients. What a pleasant way to get your vitamins!

YIELD: 8 CUPS, OR 10 WITH VODKA

8 cups V8 juice
½ cup prepared horseradish, or more to taste
2 tablespoons Worcestershire sauce
1 tablespoon Tabasco sauce, or more to taste
2 teaspoons freshly cracked black pepper
2¾ cups vodka (omit for a Virgin Mary)
Ice cubes
Celery sticks, for stirring
Lemon or lime slices

Place the V8 juice, horseradish, Worcestershire and Tabasco sauces, pepper and vodka (if using) in a large pitcher and stir well. Pour over ice and serve immediately, garnished with a celery stick and lemon slice.

Cosmopolitan

Made famous by the ladies of *Sex and the City*, this sweet/tart drink delivers a powerful punch.

> "The telephone is a good way to talk to people without having to offer them a drink."
>
> —FRAN LEBOWITZ, JOURNALIST (B. 1951)

YIELD: 6 CUPS

2 cups citron vodka
1 cup Triple Sec
1 cup Rose's Lime Juice
2 cups cranberry juice

Place all the ingredients in a pitcher and stir well. Serve in well-chilled martini glasses.

Sangría

This refreshing, fruit-infused punch is a real crowd pleaser.

> "Old wine and friends improve with age."
> —ITALIAN PROVERB

YIELD: 5½–6 CUPS

1 bottle dry red wine
1 cup fresh orange juice
2 lemons, thinly sliced
2 limes, thinly sliced
2 oranges, thinly sliced
Ice cubes
Seltzer (optional)

Place the wine, orange juice and the lemon, lime and orange slices in a pitcher and stir well. Cover and refrigerate overnight.

Pour into glasses filled with ice cubes. Add seltzer, if desired. Serve immediately.

Fruit Punch

Not too sweet, not too tart: kids and grownups alike love this simple fruit drink.

YIELD: 12 CUPS

4 cups cranberry juice
4 cups grapefruit juice
4 cups orange juice

Pour into a pitcher, stir well and refrigerate up to 5 days.

Desserts

Although I am a fan of dessert, I don't go for complicated, multilayered creations. Even when I eat at a restaurant, I want a piece of a wonderful cake or a few cookies. These recipes are all just that: simple, delicious, not showy.

Paige's Banana Bread

There is not one unusual or special ingredient in this banana bread—which was created by Paige Retus, Olives' former pastry chef—but it is, hands down, the absolute best. In fact, Todd English and I were so inspired when we tasted this bread that we decided to write *The Olives Dessert Table* with Paige. We figured if she could work this kind of magic with banana bread, she could do anything. And she can.

ALL-PURPOSE FLOUR, stored in a well-sealed container or in a resealable plastic bag, will keep in the pantry for up to 1 year and in the freezer for up to 2. Adding a few bay leaves to the bag will keep any bugs out.

YIELD: 12 SLICES

3–4 overripe bananas

1¼ cups sugar

½ cup unsalted butter, melted and slightly cooled

2 large eggs, at room temperature

1 teaspoon vanilla extract

1½ cups all-purpose flour

½ teaspoon kosher salt

1½ teaspoons baking soda

½ cup chopped toasted walnuts (page 12, optional)

Preheat the oven to 350 degrees. Lightly butter a 9 x 5 x 5-inch loaf pan.

Place the bananas and sugar in the bowl of a mixer fitted with a paddle and whip until smooth, 2–3 minutes.

Add the butter, eggs and vanilla extract, whipping well and scraping down the sides of the bowl before each addition. Scrape down the sides of the bowl and add the flour, salt, baking soda and nuts, if desired. Mix to combine.

Pour the batter into the prepared pan and transfer it to the oven. Bake until the bread is golden brown and firm in the center, about 1 hour.

Serve immediately or set aside to cool to room temperature.

Pumpkin Bread

Not surprisingly, both canned and fresh pumpkin are plentiful only in the fall, so if you're a fan of pumpkin bread, it's wise to stock up on canned pumpkin puree (not pumpkin pie filling, which has added spices and sugar in it).

BAKING POWDER and BAKING SODA stay fresh for 2 years in the pantry. To check the viability of baking powder, place ½ teaspoon in a cup of water: if it bubbles, it's still good.

> "I went to a general store but they wouldn't let me buy anything specific." —STEPHEN WRIGHT, COMEDIAN (B. 1955)

YIELD: 12 SLICES

1½ cups canned pumpkin puree

1¼ cups sugar

1¼ cups canola oil

3 large eggs

1½ cups all-purpose flour

1½ teaspoons baking powder

1½ teaspoons ground cinnamon

1 teaspoon baking soda

1 teaspoon kosher salt

Preheat the oven to 350 degrees. Lightly butter a loaf pan.

Place the pumpkin, sugar, oil and eggs in the bowl of a mixer fitted with a paddle and beat until the ingredients are incorporated, 2–3 minutes.

Scrape down the sides of the bowl and add the flour, baking powder, cinnamon, baking soda and salt. Mix until just smooth.

Pour the batter into the prepared pan and transfer it to the oven. Bake until the bread is golden brown and firm in the center, about 40 minutes.

Serve immediately or set aside to cool to room temperature.

Brown Sugar Cookies

A little more complex in flavor than a standard sugar cookie, these are loved equally by children and grown-ups.

BROWN SUGAR stays fresh for about 18 months. It turns hard when its moisture evaporates. A slice of fresh apple or a piece of bread stored with the sugar helps to keep it soft and moist. Domino Foods suggests this microwave method to soften hardened brown sugar: Put about ½ pound of hardened sugar in a microwave-safe bowl. Cover with two pieces of wet paper towel. Tightly cover the bowl with plastic wrap and heat in the microwave at full power for 1½ to 2 minutes. Fluff the sugar with a fork (the sugar will be hot). Cool slightly and use immediately.

> "C is for cookie, it's good enough for me; oh cookie cookie cookie starts with C." —"COOKIE MONSTER," ON *SESAME STREET*

YIELD: ABOUT 8 DOZEN COOKIES

1½ cups unsalted butter, at room temperature

1½ cups light brown sugar

2 large eggs, at room temperature

4 cups all-purpose flour

4 teaspoons baking soda

1 teaspoon ground ginger

2 teaspoons ground cinnamon

1 teaspoon kosher salt

Preheat the oven to 375 degrees.

Place the butter and brown sugar in the bowl of a mixer fitted with a paddle and mix until creamy. Scrape down the sides of the bowl. Add the eggs, one at a time, mixing well between additions. Add all the remaining ingredients and mix again.

(Continued on next page)

To form the cookies, break off small pieces and roll into 1-inch balls. Place 2 inches apart on an ungreased cookie sheet and bake until the edges of the cookies are just brown, 8–12 minutes. For crispy cookies, let them cool on the sheet. Let the cookie sheet cool between batches. Set aside to cool completely. Store in a resealable plastic bag for 3–4 days.

Alternatively, form the dough into four 1½-inch-diameter logs, cover them with parchment paper and then place them in a resealable plastic bag. Refrigerate up to 2 weeks and freeze up to 2 months. Cut the dough into ¼-inch slices when ready to use and proceed as above.

Citrus Shortbread

Don't be shocked by the amount of citrus zest in these cookies; if you're a fan of citrus, they're well worth the work, especially if you own a Microplane.

You can alter this recipe (and reduce your workload) by replacing the citrus zest with ½ cup unsweetened shredded coconut.

YIELD: ABOUT 6 DOZEN COOKIES

2 cups unsalted butter, at room temperature
⅔ cup confectioners' sugar
⅔ cup granulated sugar
Grated zest of 6 lemons, or of 4 lemons and 3 limes
1 tablespoon plus 1 teaspoon vanilla extract
2 teaspoons kosher salt
4½ cups all-purpose flour

Place the butter and both sugars in the bowl of a mixer fitted with a paddle, or in a food processor fitted with a steel blade, and mix until creamy. Scrape down the sides of the bowl, add all the remaining ingredients and mix again.

Form the dough into two 1½-inch-diameter logs and cover with parchment paper. Place the logs in a resealable plastic bag and refrigerate at least 1 hour and up to 1 month, or freeze up to 2 months.

Preheat the oven to 325 degrees. Line a baking sheet with parchment paper.

With the tip of a very sharp knife, cut ¼-inch slices of the dough. Place them 2 inches apart on the prepared sheet, transfer it to the oven and bake until the cookies are just beginning to brown on the edges, about 20 minutes. Let the baking sheet cool completely between batches. Set aside to cool completely. Store in a resealable plastic bag for up to 1 week.

Oatmeal Lace Cookies

A delicate, grown-up oatmeal cookie. Serve these with vanilla or coffee ice cream.

GRANULATED SUGAR and CONFECTIONERS' SUGAR will stay fresh for 2 years. If granulated sugar gets lumpy, break the lumps up with a fork, or if they are big, pulse them in a food processor. Confectioners' sugar picks up moisture easily, so be sure to store it in an airtight bag and remove all the air each time you reseal it. If it does pick up moisture and harden, throw out the hardened pieces: it's almost impossible to revive.

> "Children ask better questions than adults. 'May I have a cookie?' 'Why is the sky blue?' and 'What does a cow say?' are far more likely to elicit a cheerful response than 'Where's your manuscript?' 'Why haven't you called?' and 'Who's your lawyer?' "
>
> —FRAN LEBOWITZ, JOURNALIST (B. 1951)

YIELD: ABOUT 12 DOZEN COOKIES

2 cups unsalted butter, at room temperature

4 cups sugar

¼ cup vanilla extract

1 cup all-purpose flour

6 cups rolled oats

1 teaspoon kosher salt

Place the butter and sugar in the bowl of a mixer fitted with a paddle, or in a food processor fitted with a steel blade, and mix until creamy. Scrape down the sides of the bowl, add all the remaining ingredients and mix again. Form the dough into four 1½-inch-diameter logs, cover with parchment paper and refrigerate at least 1 hour and up to 1 week, or freeze up to 2 months.

Preheat the oven to 350 degrees. Line a baking sheet with parchment paper.

Slice the dough into ⅛-inch-thick rounds and place them 2 inches apart on the prepared sheet. Bake until golden brown throughout, 10–12 minutes. Allow the cookies to sit on the sheet for no more than 2 minutes and then transfer them to a wire rack to cool. Let the baking sheet cool between batches. Set aside to cool completely. The cookies can be stored in a resealable plastic bag for 3–4 days.

Mexican Wedding Cookies

The first time I tried these cookies, I used walnuts but thought they'd be even better with almonds or pecans. However, while both versions were first-rate, neither compared with the walnuts, which remains my favorite. These are great cookies to make when you have a few minutes to spare: the dough can be made up to 2 weeks ahead and refrigerated. Additionally, once baked, the cookies keep fresh for at least 3 days.

UNSALTED BUTTER will keep in the refrigerator up to 2 weeks past the code date and can be frozen up to 4 months.

> "All the things I really like to do are either immoral, illegal or fattening."
> —ALEXANDER WOOLLCOTT, WRITER AND CRITIC (1887–1943)

YIELD: ABOUT 10 DOZEN COOKIES

2 cups unsalted butter, at room temperature
½ cup confectioners' sugar, plus additional for rolling
2 teaspoons vanilla extract
4 cups all-purpose flour
4 cups finely ground lightly toasted walnuts (page 12)

Preheat the oven to 375 degrees.

Place the butter and sugar in the bowl of a mixer fitted with a paddle, and mix until creamy. Scrape down the sides of the bowl, add the vanilla extract and mix again. Add the flour and walnuts, mix well and scrape the bowl again.

Shape large teaspoons of the dough into little balls and place them 2 inches apart on an ungreased cookie sheet. Bake until the edges of the cookies are just brown, about 15 minutes.

Remove the cookies from the cookie sheet, cool on a wire rack, and then roll in confectioners' sugar.

Store in resealable plastic bags.

Alternatively, form the dough into four 1½-inch-diameter logs, cover with parchment paper and then place in a resealable plastic bag. Refrigerate up to 2 weeks and freeze up to 2 months. Cut the dough into 1/4-inch slices when ready to use and proceed as above.

Chocolate Chip Cookies

Who doesn't love chocolate chip cookies?

CHOCOLATE CHIPS will last up to 2 years if well wrapped and stored in a cool, dark place. If white streaks (bloom) appear on the surface, don't worry: they will disappear when cooked.

> "Think what a better world it would be if we all, the whole world, had cookies and milk about three o'clock every afternoon and then lay down on our blankets for a nap."
>
> —BARBARA JORDAN, CONGRESSWOMAN (1936–1996)

YIELD: ABOUT 12 DOZEN COOKIES

2 cups unsalted butter, at room temperature

I cup granulated sugar

2 cups light brown sugar

3 eggs, at room temperature

I tablespoon vanilla extract

2 cups rolled oats

4 cups all-purpose flour

2 teaspoons baking powder

2 teaspoons baking soda

2 teaspoons kosher salt

4 cups semisweet chocolate chips

2 cups lightly toasted pecans, walnuts or almonds, chopped (page 12)

(Continued on next page)

Preheat the oven to 325 degrees.

Place the butter and both sugars in the bowl of a mixer fitted with a paddle and mix until creamy. Scrape down the sides of the bowl. Add the eggs, one at a time, mixing well between additions. Add the remaining ingredients, mix again and scrape down the sides of the bowl.

Drop large teaspoons of the dough 2 inches apart on an ungreased cookie sheet and bake until the edges of the cookies are just brown, about 12 minutes. For crispy cookies, let them cool on the sheet. Let the cookie sheet cool between batches.

Alternatively, form the dough into four 1½-inch-diameter logs, cover with parchment paper and then place in a resealable plastic bag. Refrigerate up to 2 weeks or freeze up to 2 months. Cut the dough into 1/4-inch slices when ready to use and proceed as above.

Peanut Butter Oat Cookies

These are one of the rare cookies that taste best after they've cooled. If you can stand to wait that long, it's well worth it. If someone in your house is allergic to peanuts, these are equally delicious made with another nut butter, like cashew or almond.

Sometimes I add 1 cup sweetened shredded coconut, or replace the nut butter with ½ cup Nutella plus ¼ cup unsweetened cocoa powder. Sometimes I do both.

> "Nothing takes the taste out of peanut butter quite like unrequited love."
>
> —CHARLES SCHULTZ, CARTOONIST (1922–2000)

YIELD: ABOUT 8 DOZEN COOKIES

2 cups unsalted butter, at room temperature

1 cup granulated sugar

2 cups light brown sugar

2 cups peanut, almond, or cashew butter

4 large eggs, at room temperature

2 tablespoons vanilla extract

3 cups rolled oats, ground if desired

4 cups all-purpose flour

1 tablespoon plus 1 teaspoon baking soda

2 teaspoons kosher salt

Preheat the oven to 350 degrees. Lightly grease a cookie sheet and line it with parchment paper.

Place the butter and both sugars in the bowl of a mixer fitted with a paddle and mix until smooth. Scrape down the sides of the bowl. Add the peanut butter, eggs and vanilla extract and mix until just combined, being careful not to overbeat. Scrape down the sides of the bowl. Add the oats, flour, baking soda and salt and mix until everything is well incorporated.

Place teaspoonfuls of the dough 2 inches apart on the prepared cookie sheet and transfer it to the oven. Bake until the edges of the cookies are beginning to firm up, about 15 minutes. For crispy cookies, let them cool on the sheet. Let the cookie sheet cool between batches.

Alternatively, form the dough into four 1½-inch-diameter logs, cover with parchment paper and then place in a resealable plastic bag. Refrigerate up to 2 weeks and freeze up to 2 months. Cut the dough into 1/4-inch slices when ready to use and proceed as above.

Baked Apples

Even when it's topped with vanilla ice cream, whipped cream or just a drizzle of heavy cream, I feel virtuous digging into one of these apples.

Purchase APPLES that are firm to the touch and that have no visible brown spots or holes in the skin. Apples should be stored in the refrigerator to prevent them from overripening. Most varieties can stay fresh for up to 6 weeks.

> "Comfort me with apples: for I am sick of love."
>
> —THE SONG OF SOLOMON 2:5

TO MAKE A LEMON STRIP: Using a vegetable peeler, remove 1½–1¾ inches lemon zest, making sure you don't include any of the white pith.

SERVES 4

2–4 tablespoons maple syrup, light brown sugar or honey

½ teaspoon ground cinnamon

¼ cup raisins, craisins or currants

¼ cup lightly toasted walnuts, coarsely chopped (page 12)

2 strips lemon zest, minced or chopped

4 Granny Smith apples, top third cut off and discarded, cored

2 tablespoons unsalted butter, cut into little pieces

6 tablespoons dry white wine, apple juice or orange juice

Preheat the oven to 375 degrees.

Place the maple syrup, cinnamon, raisins, walnuts and lemon zest in a small bowl and mix well. Divide the mixture evenly and stuff it inside the apples. Place the apples in a small baking dish, touching each other, top with pieces of butter and surround with the wine.

Transfer to the oven and bake until the apples are soft, about 1 hour. Serve immediately or at room temperature.

Burnt Caramel Sauce

A few years ago, my brother Tom was bemoaning spending so much money at Starbucks to simply add caramel sauce to his coffee. I told him it was simple and that if he got me the ingredients, I would show him how. He went out and purchased heavy cream and when he returned home, I started cooking. I got distracted and when I smelled the burnt sugar, I decided that since it was merely a demo, it didn't really matter and continued with the recipe. When I was finished, I wondered if the sauce would taste any good. It was amazing. That was my summer of burnt caramel: I made it constantly and drizzled it on coffee ice cream every night (it wasn't bad on vanilla either). It's delicious on Baked Apples (page 272) too, and a drizzle over Rice Pudding (page 288) turns an everyday dessert into something very special.

YIELD: 2½ CUPS

1½ cups sugar
2 tablespoons water
2 cups heavy cream
2 teaspoons vanilla extract
½ teaspoon kosher salt

Place the sugar and water in a saucepan and bring to a boil. Continue boiling, without stirring, until it begins to color at the edges, 2–3 minutes. Cook, whisking all the while, until the syrup turns a deep brown and just begins to smell burnt, about an additional 2 minutes. (The darker the syrup, the deeper the burn, so cook accordingly.)

Slowly add the cream, continuing to whisk, until it is completely incorporated.

Off heat, add the vanilla extract and salt. Cool to room temperature then cover and refrigerate up to 2 weeks.

Fruit Crisp

If this were the only dessert I could ever have again, I would be completely satisfied. In fact, I would be thrilled. My favorite combination is strawberry-rhubarb, but I try not to make it too often because I am incapable of stopping myself from eating it. I like to serve it warm: I take a normal-size piece and then a tiny sliver and then another tiny sliver and later, when I have cleaned up after dinner, I eat another piece cold. And then the next day I eat some more. I am never ever sick of it.

The proportions in the mixed fruit combinations are entirely up to your personal taste.

> "You have to eat oatmeal or you'll dry up. Anybody knows that."
> —KAY THOMPSON, AUTHOR OF *ELOISE* (1905–1998)

MAKES 2 CRISPS; EACH SERVES 6–8

For the fruit:

12 cups chopped pitted peaches, or prune plums, or apples, or
    apples and cranberries, or, peaches and blueberries, or
    blueberries and rhubarb, or strawberries and rhubarb
2 tablespoons sugar
2 tablespoons all-purpose flour

For the topping:

1½ cups all-purpose flour
1½ cups rolled oats
1 cup chopped lightly toasted pecans or walnuts (page 12, optional)
6 tablespoons granulated sugar
½ cup light brown sugar
¾ teaspoon kosher salt
¾ cup unsalted butter, melted

Preheat the oven to 375 degrees.

TO PREPARE THE FRUIT: Place the fruit, sugar and flour in a large bowl and toss well. Divide equally between two 8 x 8-inch baking pans.

TO PREPARE THE TOPPING: Place the flour, oats, nuts, if desired, both sugars and salt in a large mixing bowl and toss well. Add the butter and toss again until it forms a consistent texture. Spread the topping evenly between the two pans.

Place the pans in the oven and cook until the crisps are lightly browned on top, 35–45 minutes. Serve warm, at room temperature or cooled.

(You can bake one and freeze one: Cover the second pan with aluminum foil and freeze up to one month. Thaw frozen crisp, then follow baking instructions above.)

Peach Pie

Though most of the peaches in my house don't last long enough to be cooked, when they do, this is where they end up.

> "An apple is an excellent thing—until you have tried a peach!"
> —GEORGE DU MAURIER, WRITER (1834–1896)

SERVES 6–8

For the pastry:

3 cups all-purpose flour

¾ teaspoon kosher salt

1 tablespoon sugar

1 cup unsalted butter, chilled, cut into thin slices

4–6 tablespoons ice water

For the filling:

8 perfectly ripe peaches, thinly sliced

1 cup sour cream or full-fat yogurt

¼ cup brown sugar

1 tablespoon all-purpose flour

1 teaspoon vanilla extract

TO MAKE THE PASTRY: Place the flour, salt and sugar in a food processor fitted with a steel blade and pulse to combine. Add the butter, 1 slice at a time, and process until the mixture is crumbly and there are no clumps of butter left. Add the ice water and process until a ball forms, about 30 seconds. Form the dough into two disks, wrap them in plastic wrap or waxed paper and refrigerate until firm, at least 1 hour, or freeze up to 2 weeks in a resealable plastic bag.

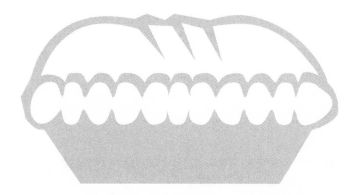

On a generously floured surface, roll out each disk out into a 12-inch circle and gently place one in a 9- or 9½-inch pie pan. Place the remaining circle on a sheet of waxed paper and refrigerate until ready to use.

Preheat the oven to 400 degrees.

TO PREPARE THE FILLING: Place the peaches, sour cream, sugar, flour and vanilla extract in a bowl and mix well.

Pour the filling mixture into the prepared pie shell and cover with the remaining crust. Flute the edges.

Transfer the pie to the oven and bake for 15 minutes. Lower the heat to 350 degrees and bake until the crust is golden brown and the fruit is bubbling, about 1¼ hours.

Serve hot or at room temperature.

Chocolate Chip Pie

Chocolate Chip Pie—what a concept! Like a pecan pie in texture and an undercooked chocolate chip cookie in flavor, it is a five-year-old's dream.

While I think this pie is perfect as is, there are those who wouldn't mind a scoop of ice cream or a dollop of whipped cream on top.

> "A boy doesn't have to go to war to be a hero; he can say he doesn't like pie when he sees there isn't enough to go around."
>
> —EDGAR WATSON HOWE, EDITOR AND WRITER (1853–1937)

MAKES 2 PIES; EACH SERVES 8

For the pastry:

3 cups all-purpose flour

¾ teaspoon kosher salt

2 tablespoons sugar

1 cup unsalted butter, chilled, cut into small pieces

5–6 tablespoons ice water

For the filling:

10 tablespoons (½ cup plus 2 tablespoons) unsalted butter, melted and cooled

5 large eggs, at room temperature

1 tablespoon vanilla extract

2½ cups light brown sugar

1¼ cups all-purpose flour

2¼ cups lightly toasted chopped pecans or walnuts (page 12)

2¼ cups semisweet chocolate chips

TO PREPARE THE PASTRY: Place the flour, salt and sugar in a food processor and process until combined. Add the butter, little by little, and process until pebbly. Gradually add the ice water and process until the dough pulls away from the sides. Divide the dough into two disks, cover with waxed paper and refrigerate until ready to use, at least 1 hour. (If you are not going to use the dough within 1 day, double-wrap, first in waxed paper, then in foil, and freeze.)

Preheat the oven to 350 degrees.

On a generously floured surface, roll out each disk into a 12-inch circle and place each one in a 9-inch pie pan.

Prick the bottom with a fork and line it with either parchment paper or aluminum foil. Place pie weights or beans on the paper, press down, and transfer to the oven. Bake for 10 minutes; then remove the paper and weights and cook for an additional 5 minutes. Set aside to cool.

TO PREPARE THE FILLING: Place all the filling ingredients in a large bowl and mix until well combined. Pour half of the filling into each cooked pie shell and transfer them to the oven. Bake until golden brown, about 40 minutes.

Serve immediately or at room temperature; or cool, wrap well with plastic wrap and set aside for up to 3 days.

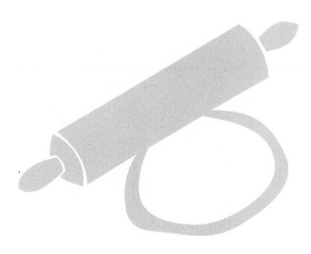

Dain Fritz's Grandmother's Carrot Cake with Cream Cheese Frosting

I love the pure sweet flavor of this cake. I have been making it for thirty years and for every occasion; it's the rare recipe I never mess with.

Although I almost always use the cream cheese frosting, it's also good with just a dusting of confectioners' sugar.

> "Vegetables are a must on a diet. I suggest carrot cake, zucchini bread, and pumpkin pie."
>
> —JIM DAVIS, CARTOONIST (B. 1945)

SERVES 8–12

For the cake:

3 cups grated carrots

1 cup canola oil

2 cups sugar

4 large eggs, at room temperature

2 cups all-purpose flour

2 teaspoons baking soda

1 teaspoon kosher salt

½ teaspoon ground cinnamon

For the Cream Cheese Frosting:

¼ pounds cream cheese, at room temperature

½ cup confectioners' sugar

1 teaspoon vanilla extract

1 cup lightly toasted walnuts or pecans, chopped (page 12, optional)

Preheat the oven to 350 degrees. Lightly grease and flour a Bundt pan or a 9 x 13-inch baking pan.

TO MAKE THE CAKE: Place the carrots, oil, sugar and eggs in a mixer fitted with a paddle, and blend until well incorporated. Add the flour, baking soda, salt and cinnamon, and mix until well incorporated. Pour the batter into the prepared pan, transfer to the oven and bake for 40 minutes. Set the cake aside to cool. (If you are using a Bundt pan, allow the cake to cool in the pan at least 45 minutes. Turn the cake onto a serving dish and allow to cool completely before frosting. If using a 9 x 13-inch pan, allow the cake to cool in the pan, then cover with the frosting.)

While the cake is baking, PREPARE THE FROSTING: Place the cream cheese in a mixer fitted with a paddle and blend until softened. Add the sugar and vanilla extract and blend.

When the cake has cooled, spread it with the icing. Sprinkle with the nuts, if desired.

Walnut Rum Cake

Boozy, rich and unforgettable. Definitely *not* for the kids.

> "I'd love a piece of fruit, but I'd just as soon eat a piece of cake."
> —SHIRLEY MACLAINE, ACTRESS (B. 1934)

SERVES 8–12

For the cake:

1 cup unsalted butter, at room temperature

2 cups sugar

2 large eggs, at room temperature

1 teaspoon vanilla extract

2½ cups all-purpose flour

2 teaspoons baking powder

1 teaspoon ground cinnamon

1 teaspoon baking soda

¼ teaspoon kosher salt

½ cup dark rum

1 cup buttermilk or full-fat plain yogurt

2⅓ cups lightly toasted walnuts, finely chopped (page 12)

For the soaking syrup:

½ cup sugar

¼ cup water

¼ cup dark rum

¼ cup orange juice

¼ cup fresh lemon juice

Confectioners' sugar, for garnish

Preheat the oven 350 degrees. Lightly butter and flour a 9-inch Bundt pan.

TO MAKE THE CAKE: Place the butter and sugar in the bowl of a mixer fitted with a paddle and beat until well creamed, 3–5 minutes. Add the eggs and vanilla and beat again.

Place the flour, baking powder, cinnamon, baking soda and salt in a bowl and toss to combine. Add the flour mixture to the butter mixture in three additions, alternating with the rum and buttermilk and scraping down the sides of the bowl between additions. Add the nuts and mix again.

Pour the batter into the prepared pan, transfer it to the oven and bake until a tester comes out clean, 45–60 minutes. Set aside to cool for 5 minutes, then remove it from the pan.

While the cake is baking, PREPARE THE SOAKING SYRUP: Place the sugar and water in a small saucepan and bring to a boil over high heat for 2 minutes. Add the rum and juices and cook until heated throughout, about 1 minute.

Invert the cake by placing it back in the pan and prick the surface of the cake with a toothpick. Brush on the hot soaking syrup and then let the cake cool to room temperature. Cover with plastic wrap and set aside for 2 days, turning the cake over every half day or so.

Sprinkle with confectioners' sugar just before serving.

Banana Cake with Dark Chocolate Ganache

Bananas and chocolate are an inspired combination. This light and tender banana cake is frosted with a luscious chocolate ganache: heaven.

> "All I need is a little love now and then, but some chocolate will do for now."
>
> —CHARLES SCHULTZ, CARTOONIST (1922–2000)

SERVES 8–12

For the cake:

1 cup unsalted butter, at room temperature

2 cups sugar

3 large eggs, at room temperature

1 tablespoon vanilla extract

3–4 overripe bananas, mashed with a fork

3 cups all-purpose flour

1¼ teaspoons baking powder

¾ teaspoon baking soda

1 teaspoon kosher salt

¾ cup buttermilk or sour cream

For the ganache:

2 cups semisweet chocolate chips

1 cup heavy cream

Preheat the oven to 350 degrees. Lightly butter a 9 x 13-inch baking pan.

TO MAKE THE CAKE: Place the butter and sugar in the bowl of a mixer fitted with a paddle, and beat until well creamed, 3–5 minutes. Add the eggs, vanilla and bananas and beat again.

Place the flour, baking powder, baking soda and salt in a bowl and toss to combine. Add the flour mixture to the butter mixture in three additions, alternating with the buttermilk and scraping down the sides of the bowl between additions.

Place the batter in the prepared pan, transfer it to the oven and bake until the top is golden brown and a tester comes out clean, about 45 minutes. Set it aside to cool. When it has cooled, remove it from the pan.

While the cake is cooling, MAKE THE GANACHE: Place the chocolate chips in the top of a double boiler over medium heat and cook until the chocolate has melted. Off heat, very, very gradually pour in the cream, stirring continuously until it is smooth. Set aside to cool.

When both the cake and the ganache have cooled, ice the cake: Using a thin spatula, generously cover the top of the cake with the icing. Serve immediately!

Bread Pudding with Whiskey Sauce

Homey, yummy classic bread pudding with a grown-up twist. You can always serve it with ice cream or whipped cream for the kids.

I recently tried this with the addition of very high quality chunks of bittersweet chocolate. They didn't melt completely but instead stayed as chunks. Yum.

SERVES 8–12

For the bread pudding:

1 large loaf stale French bread, cubed, or 5–6 stale croissants, cut up

4 cups whole milk

3 large eggs

1½ cups sugar

½–¾ cup raisins or dried cranberries (optional)

2 teaspoons vanilla extract

For the whiskey sauce:

YIELD: 1½ CUPS

½ cup unsalted butter

1 cup sugar

1 large egg, lightly beaten

½ cup bourbon

TO MAKE THE PUDDING: Preheat the oven to 325 degrees. Lightly butter a 9 x 13-inch baking dish.

Place the bread cubes in a bowl and cover with the milk. Let stand until all the milk is absorbed, about 10 minutes.

Place the eggs and sugar in another bowl and beat until smooth. Stir in the raisins, if desired, and the vanilla extract. Pour the egg mixture over the bread and mix well.

Pour the mixture into the prepared baking dish and bake until brown and set, about 1 hour.

TO MAKE THE WHISKEY SAUCE: While the pudding is baking, place the butter in a small saucepan over low heat. When it has melted, add the sugar and stir until it is completely dissolved. Set aside to cool for 5 minutes. Then add the egg and whisk until the mixture is room temperature. Add the bourbon and bring the mixture to a boil. Serve hot or cold, over warm pudding.

Rice Pudding

Old-fashioned, creamy and luscious, this is perfect following a spicy meal, particularly Jamaican Jerk Chicken (page 160) or Spicy Mustard Flank Steaks (page 198).

I'm a purist and prefer this pudding as is. However, if you are looking for a little variety, when you add the vanilla, you can add ¼–½ cup chopped lightly toasted pecans, walnuts or pistachios or thinly sliced almonds, and/or ½ cup raisins, currants, dried cranberries or cherries, or diced apricots or prunes.

> "One of the secrets of a long and fruitful life is to forgive everybody everything before you go to bed."
>
> —ANN LANDERS, ADVICE COLUMNIST (1918–2002)

SERVES 6–8

2 cups water

1 cup jasmine rice

¼ teaspoon kosher salt

3½ cups whole milk

¾ cup heavy cream

¾ cup sugar

1 teaspoon vanilla extract

1 teaspoon ground cinnamon

Place the water in a medium-size saucepan and bring to a boil over high heat. Add the rice and salt and return to a boil. Lower the heat to low, cover, and simmer, stirring every 5 minutes, until the rice is almost tender, about 10 minutes.

Add the milk, cream and sugar and cook, stirring frequently, until almost all the liquid has been absorbed, about 30 minutes. Stir in the vanilla extract and pour the mixture into a 9 x 13-inch baking pan. Sprinkle with the cinnamon and let cool to room temperature.

Serve immediately, or cover the surface tightly with plastic wrap and refrigerate up to 2 days.

Ricotta Cake with Nuts and Lemon

This is a lighter, airier, more delicate version of cheesecake. If you're a fan of ricotta cheese, as I am, you'll love this.

HONEY will keep indefinitely in a cool, dry place, although it may crystallize and harden. If that happens, put the opened jar in a pan of hot water and let it heat gently until dissolved. Or microwave the opened jar on full power for 15 to 60 seconds.

> "You can't have your cake and eat it too."
> —PROVERB

SERVES 8

2 pounds skim-milk ricotta cheese

½ cup finely ground gingersnaps, molasses cookies, graham crackers, toasted bread crumbs, *or* lightly toasted hazelnuts, pecans or walnuts, *or* a combination of any of the above

5 large egg yolks, at room temperature, beaten

1 teaspoon finely chopped lemon zest

½ cup sugar

1¼ teaspoons vanilla extract

Honey, for drizzling

Line a small colander with muslin or a strong paper towel. Add the ricotta and place the colander over a bowl. Cover with plastic wrap and refrigerate for at least 4 hours and up to 24 hours.

Preheat the oven to 325 degrees.

Lightly butter a 9- or 10-inch springform pan and line the pan with the ground cookie crumbs and/or nuts.

Discard the liquid that has drained through the colander. Place the drained ricotta,

(Continued on next page)

egg yolks, lemon zest, sugar and vanilla extract in a bowl and mix until smooth. Pour into the prepared pan. Transfer the pan to the oven and bake until the top is slightly golden and tiny bubbles start to appear on the surface, about 35 minutes. Do not over-bake.

Set the cake aside until it starts to pull away from the sides of the pan, about 10 minutes.

Remove the pan sides and let the cake cool. Cover and refrigerate at least 4 hours and up to 24 hours. Serve, drizzled with honey.

Cheesecake

This is a very creamy, smooth cheesecake, based on the classic New York version. Fresh berries are a refreshing contrast to the richness of the cheesecake.

SERVES 8–12

For the crust:

1¼ cups ground graham crackers or gingersnaps
¼ cup confectioners' sugar
5 tablespoons unsalted butter, melted

For the cream cheese layer:

2 large eggs
¾ pound cream cheese
½ cup granulated sugar
½ teaspoon vanilla extract
1 teaspoon fresh lemon juice
½ teaspoon kosher salt

For the sour cream layer:

1½ cups sour cream
2 tablespoons granulated sugar
½ teaspoon vanilla extract
⅛ teaspoon kosher salt

Fresh raspberries, strawberries and/or blueberries, for garnish

TO MAKE THE CRUST: Place the cookie crumbs, sugar and butter in a medium-size mixing bowl and mix until combined. Press the mixture into a 9-inch pie pan. Cover and refrigerate at least 2 hours and up to 2 days.

(Continued on next page)

Preheat the oven to 375 degrees.

TO MAKE THE CREAM CHEESE LAYER: Place all the ingredients in a food processor or mixer and process until combined. Pour the mixture into the crust, transfer it to the oven, and bake for 20 minutes. Set it aside to cool.

While the cream cheese layer is cooling, **PREPARE THE SOUR CREAM LAYER:** Place the sour cream, sugar, vanilla extract and salt in a food processor or mixer, and process until well mixed. Pour the sour cream mixture over the cooled cream cheese layer, cover, and refrigerate at least overnight and up to 3 days.

Serve chilled or at room temperature, garnished with fresh berries.

> "A compromise is the art of dividing a cake in such a way that every-one believes he has the biggest piece."
> —LUDWIG ERHARD, ECONOMIST AND STATESMAN (1897–1977)

Breakfast/ Brunch

Other than the typical smoothie, eggs, toast or cereal, I rarely make breakfast or brunch. Perhaps that's why I love it so; its very novelty makes it one of my favorite meals.

Three Breakfast Butters

These butters can gild scones, pancakes, waffles, croissants or just plain toast. They can be shaped into cylinders, covered in waxed paper and placed in a resealable plastic bag, then refrigerated or frozen. Slice them into coins for a nice presentation.

> "Why, sometimes I've believed as many as six impossible things before breakfast."
>
> — LEWIS CARROLL, WRITER (1832–1898)

YIELD: ½ CUP FLAVORED BUTTER

Honey Butter

½ cup unsalted butter, at room temperature

3 tablespoons honey

¼ teaspoon vanilla extract

Apricot Butter

½ cup unsalted butter, at room temperature

2 teaspoons apricot jam, or any good quality jam or preserves (but not jelly)

Cinnamon Sugar Butter

½ cup unsalted butter, at room temperature
1 teaspoon ground cinnamon
2 tablespoons light brown sugar

Place the butter in a small bowl and mash until smooth. Add the remaining ingredients and mix until combined. Place on a large piece of waxed paper and form into a log. Use immediately, cover and refrigerate 2 weeks, or freeze up to 2 months.

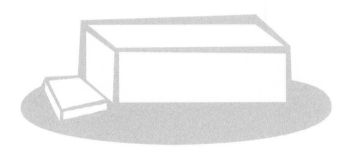

Four Cream Cheeses

These cream cheeses really wake up a plain toasted bagel. Try them on toast and Biscuits (page 299) too. For an easy hors d'oeuvre, smear some of the chive or herb cream cheese on a cracker and top it with a bit of smoked salmon.

> "The bagel is a lonely roll to eat all by yourself because in order for the true taste to come out you need your family. One to cut the bagels, one to toast them, one to put on the cream cheese and the lox, one to put them on the table and one to supervise."
>
> —GERTRUDE BERG, ACTRESS (1899–1966)

YIELD: 1 POUND FLAVORED CREAM CHEESE

Chive Cream Cheese

1 pound cream cheese, at room temperature

2 tablespoons buttermilk

⅓–½ cup finely chopped fresh chives

Herb Cream Cheese

1 pound cream cheese, at room temperature

2 tablespoons buttermilk

⅓ cup finely chopped fresh herbs, including any combination of basil, dill, parsley, mint and cilantro leaves

Raspberry Cream Cheese

1 pound cream cheese, at room temperature

2 tablespoons buttermilk

2 tablespoons raspberry jam or any good quality jam or preserves (but not jelly)

Honey Cream Cheese

1 pound cream cheese, at room temperature
2 tablespoons buttermilk
2 tablespoons honey

Place the cream cheese and the other ingredients in a bowl and mash with a fork until well combined. Serve immediately, or cover and refrigerate up to 3 days.

Fresh Fruit Salad

Honestly, it would be silly to write a recipe for fruit salad. Just use the freshest fruit you can find and let your taste and imagination guide you. Try some of the ideas below.

> "When one has tasted watermelon one knows what angels eat."
> —MARK TWAIN, HUMORIST, WRITER AND LECTURER (1835–1910)

All berries (strawberries, blueberries, blackberries, raspberries)

All melon (watermelon, cantaloupe, honeydew, Crenshaw)

Mixed melons and berries

Winter fruits: apples, pears, grapes and bananas

Tropical fruits: mangoes, pineapple, papayas and kiwi

Blueberries, bananas and peaches

Apricots, plums and blueberries

Pineapple, bananas and strawberries

Red fruits: red grapes, plums, and strawberries

WHAT DO YOU DO TO MAKE YOUR FRUIT SALAD MORE THAN JUST A BOWL OF CUT-UP FRUIT? ADD:

Equal amounts of lemon juice and confectioners' sugar

Fresh mint leaves

Diced dried fruit

Lightly toasted nuts

Lime juice and coconut

Sour cream and brown sugar

Balsamic vinegar on berries

Honey and yogurt

Champagne or sparkling cider

Sour cream and mint

Biscuits

These craggy biscuits are equally at home on the dinner table (particularly with stews) or at breakfast (served with flavored butters). Either way, if you eat them as soon as they come out of the oven (when they're at their finest), be prepared to eat too many. And don't be tempted to shape these; they're best when handled as little as possible.

YIELD: 12 BISCUITS

3 cups all-purpose flour

I tablespoon sugar

I tablespoon baking powder

I teaspoon kosher salt

I teaspoon baking soda

¾ cup unsalted butter, chilled or frozen, cut into thin slices

I cup buttermilk, plain full-fat yogurt or sour cream

Preheat the oven to 425 degrees. Line a baking sheet with parchment paper.

Place the flour, sugar, baking powder, salt and baking soda in a food processor fitted with a steel blade and mix to combine. While the processor is running, add the butter, a few slices at a time, and process until the mixture resembles cornmeal. Transfer the mixture to a large mixing bowl. Add the buttermilk and mix *by hand* until combined. Divide the mixture into 12 pieces and place them on the prepared baking sheet. Transfer to oven and bake until golden brown, 12–15 minutes.

Serve immediately.

Hash Browns/Home Fries

A cross between home fries and hash browns, these potatoes are a great breakfast/brunch dish.

> "There is a vast difference between the savage and the civilised man, but it is never apparent to their wives until after breakfast."
>
> —HELEN ROWLAND, WRITER (1876–1950)

SERVES 4

3 cups diced Idaho, baking or Yukon potatoes (about 1½ pounds)
2 tablespoons olive oil
3 cups diced Spanish or red onions
½ teaspoon dried thyme
1 teaspoon kosher salt
1 tablespoon unsalted butter
½ teaspoon black pepper
1 tablespoon finely chopped fresh Italian flat-leaf parsley leaves,
    for garnish (optional)

Place the potatoes in a medium-size saucepan, cover with cold water and bring to a boil over high heat for 5 minutes. Drain, then rinse with cold water. Transfer to a medium-size bowl.

Place a skillet over medium heat and when it is hot, add the oil. Add the onions and cook, stirring occasionally, until they are soft and caramelized, about 25 minutes. Add them to the potatoes, and add the thyme and salt. Cover and refrigerate at least 4 hours and up to overnight.

Place a large skillet over medium heat and when it is hot, add the butter. Add the onion-potato mixture, in a single layer, and press it down as flat as possible, using a spatula. Cook for 10 minutes without stirring. Carefully turn the potatoes with the spatula and press down. Cook for 20 minutes longer, turning every 5 minutes. Add the pepper and serve immediately, garnished with the parsley, if desired.

Louisiana French Toast

A fancy name for fancy French toast and a great use for day-old croissants.

SERVES: 8–10

8 large eggs, beaten

1 cup whole milk, *or* ½ cup whole milk and ½ cup heavy cream

2 teaspoons vanilla extract

1 teaspoon ground cinnamon

2 tablespoons grated orange zest

¼ cup Grand Marnier

1 loaf challah or large French bread, cut into slices 1–1½ inches thick
      or 8 croissants, cut in half lengthwise

2 tablespoons unsalted butter

Confectioners' sugar, for garnish

Melted unsalted butter, for serving

Maple syrup, for serving

1 orange, sliced, for garnish

Preheat the oven to 200 degrees.

Place the eggs, milk, vanilla extract, cinnamon, orange zest and Grand Marnier in a large flat-bottomed bowl and whisk until frothy. Dip the bread slices in the bowl and submerge until they are saturated with the egg mixture, about 30 seconds. Set the bread aside on a large plate.

Place a large skillet over medium heat and when it is very hot, add the butter. Add a few bread slices and cook until well browned, 1–2 minutes per side. Repeat until all the bread has been cooked. Place the cooked pieces in the oven to keep warm while finishing.

Sprinkle the French toast with confectioners' sugar and serve immediately, with butter and maple syrup. Garnish with orange slices.

German Apple Pancake

When I was in high school, my mother's stepmother, Dottie, came to stay with us. On the first morning of her visit, she jumped out of bed and whipped up German Apple Pancakes, a treat I had not experienced before. I have been trying to re-create them ever since.

> "The laziest man I ever met put popcorn in his pancakes so they would turn over by themselves."
>
> —W. C. FIELDS, COMEDIAN AND ACTOR (1880–1946)

SERVES 3–4

For the apples:

2 tablespoons unsalted butter
2 Granny Smith apples, peeled and thinly sliced
2 tablespoons light brown sugar

For the batter:

3 large eggs
½ cup whole milk
½ teaspoon vanilla extract
½ cup all-purpose flour
¼ teaspoon kosher salt

Confectioners' sugar, for garnish

Preheat the oven to 450 degrees.

TO PREPARE THE APPLES: Place a 10- or 12-inch ovenproof skillet over medium heat and add the butter. When it has melted, add the apples and brown sugar and cook until golden, 15–20 minutes. Do not stir often. (This can be made 24 hours in advance, stored in the refrigerator, and gently reheated before cooking.)

While the apples are cooking, PREPARE THE BATTER: Place the eggs, milk and vanilla extract in a large bowl and mix well. Add the flour and salt and stir until smooth.

Pour the batter over the cooked apples and transfer the skillet to the oven. Bake until the pancake has puffed up and is golden brown, about 15 minutes. Remove it from the oven and sprinkle with confectioners' sugar. Serve immediately from the skillet.

Cranberry Coffee Cake

From the first time I made this seasonal rendition of a classic coffee cake, I have been eating far too much of it. It's especially hard to resist when it's warm, when it's cooling . . . and when it's cold. There's something about the fresh cranberries that makes it special, but you can substitute blueberries or even leave them out entirely (and cut 10 minutes off the cooking time).

This is especially great for holiday mornings: You can prepare the batter and the streusel topping the night before and store them separately, covered, in the refrigerator. In the morning, put the cake together and bake. I keep several bags of cranberries in the freezer to extend the season. (I even make this in the summer.)

YIELD: ABOUT 24 PIECES

For the cake:

½ cup unsalted butter, at room temperature
1 cup sugar
2 large eggs
1 teaspoon vanilla extract
2 cups all-purpose flour
1 teaspoon baking powder
1 teaspoon baking soda
½ teaspoon kosher salt
1 cup sour cream
2½ cups cranberries

For the streusel topping:

¾ cup light brown sugar
½ cup all-purpose flour
2 teaspoons ground cinnamon
¼ cup unsalted butter, cut into pieces
½ cup walnuts, coarsely chopped

Preheat the oven to 350 degrees. Butter and lightly flour a 9 x 13-inch baking pan.

TO PREPARE THE CAKE BATTER: Place the butter and sugar in the bowl of a mixer fitted with a paddle and beat until well creamed, 3–5 minutes. Scrape down the sides of the bowl, add the eggs and vanilla extract and beat again.

Add the flour, baking powder, baking soda and salt. Add the sour cream and mix until smooth. Spread the batter in the prepared pan and top it with the cranberries.

TO MAKE THE TOPPING: Place the brown sugar, flour and cinnamon in a small mixing bowl and toss to combine. Add the butter and mix until crumbly. Add the walnuts and mix well. Sprinkle the topping over the cranberries.

Transfer the pan to the oven and bake until a tester comes out clean, about 45 minutes. Serve warm or at room temperature.

Swedish Pancakes

I like to have my friends test prospective recipes, particularly on their unsuspecting children; kids often seem more open-minded when the recipe isn't part of their own family's repertoire. Twelve-year-old Charlie Steinberg isn't exactly known for his eating prowess, but I had a good feeling about these pancakes. I told him I really wanted him to be honest and that he needn't worry about my feelings if he didn't like them. He was adamant: "I swear," he proclaimed, "I love them. They're even better than Grandma's and hers are the best in Vermont." Sorry, Barbara.

SERVES 4–6

6 large eggs, at room temperature, separated
2–3 tablespoons sugar
1 teaspoon vanilla extract
2 cups milk
2 tablespoons unsalted butter, melted
½ teaspoon kosher salt
1½ cups all-purpose flour
1 tablespoon unsalted butter, for cooking
Confectioners' sugar, for garnish

Preheat the oven to 200 degrees.

Place the egg yolks, sugar and vanilla extract in a large bowl and mix well. Add the milk, melted butter and salt and mix well. Add the flour and stir well until it forms a smooth batter.

In a separate bowl, beat the egg whites until they form stiff peaks. Gently add the whites to the flour mixture.

Place a large cast-iron skillet or flat griddle over medium heat and when it is hot, add the butter. Place a drop of water on the pan and when it sizzles, pour tablespoons of the batter on the skillet and cook until lightly browned on both sides, 3–5 minutes total. Place the cooked pancakes in the oven to keep warm while finishing.

Sprinkle with lots of confectioners' sugar and serve immediately.

Scrambled Eggs with Tomatoes and Goat Cheese

Although this makes a great breakfast or brunch dish, it's also an easy supper on nights when it's just too hot or too much trouble to turn on the oven.

> "Eggs are very much like small boys. If you overheat them or over-beat them, they will turn on you, and no amount of future love will right the wrong."
>
> — ANONYMOUS

SERVES 4

¼ cup sliced scallions

1–2 garlic cloves, minced

1 beefsteak tomato, cored and diced

10–12 large eggs, beaten

¼ cup chopped fresh basil or mint leaves

¼ cup goat cheese, in several dollops or slices

1 teaspoon kosher salt

½ teaspoon black pepper

1 tablespoon unsalted butter

4 fresh mint sprigs, for garnish (optional)

Place all the ingredients except the butter and mint in a large bowl, and mix to combine. Place a 9- or 10-inch nonstick skillet over medium-low heat and when it is hot, add the butter. Add the egg mixture and cook for 1–2 minutes. Gently flip portions of the eggs, so that you do not scramble the eggs but rather gently toss them. When they are fully cooked, divide the eggs among 4 heated plates. Serve immediately, garnished with mint springs, if desired.

Scrambled Eggs with Indian Spices and Spinach

This is one of my favorite brunch items, but it's also sublime for dinner. The first time I served it for dinner, my children turned their noses up, but after they tasted it, they promptly begged me to make it again, right then and there (which I did).

EGG CARTONS have two dates on them: the day they were washed, graded and packed (the "Julian date"), which is based on the calendar: January 1 is 1 and December 31 is 365. There also is a "sell-by," or expiration, date; eggs are considered fine up to 3 weeks after their expiration date.

> "A true friend is someone who thinks that you are a good egg even though he knows that you are slightly cracked."
>
> —BERNARD MELTZER, LAWYER (B. 1914)

SERVES 2–3

3 teaspoons vegetable oil

1 small Spanish onion, halved and thinly sliced or chopped

1 garlic clove, minced

1 quarter-size slice fresh gingerroot, minced

½–1 small chile pepper, minced (optional)

1½ teaspoons curry powder, or more to taste

5–6 large eggs, beaten

1–1¼ cups packed fresh flat-leaf spinach (5–6 ounces), stems removed, leaves chopped

½ teaspoon kosher salt

2 tablespoons lightly toasted slivered almonds (page 12), for garnish

2 tablespoons lightly toasted unsweetened shredded coconut, for garnish

Lime or lemon wedges, for garnish

TO TOAST THE COCONUT: Preheat the oven to 200 degrees. Place coconut on a baking sheet, transfer to the oven, and bake until golden brown, about 10 minutes.

Place a 9- or 10-inch nonstick skillet over medium-low heat and when it is hot, add 2 teaspoons oil. Add the onion, garlic, ginger and, if desired, the chile pepper. Cook, stirring occasionally, until the onion is fragrant, soft and slightly caramelized, 7–8 minutes. Add the curry powder and cook for 1 minute. Set aside to cool slightly.

Place the eggs, spinach and salt in a small bowl and mix well. The mixture will look very spinach-y and not very egg-y. Add the onion mixture and mix well. (The eggs can be completed up to this point the night before. Simply cover and refrigerate.)

Wash and reheat the skillet, and when it is hot, add the remaining 1 teaspoon oil. Add the egg mixture and let cook for 1–2 minutes. Gently flip portions of the eggs, so that you do not scramble the eggs but rather gently toss them. When they are fully cooked, divide the eggs between 2 or 3 heated plates. Serve immediately, garnished with the almonds, coconut and lime wedges.

Frittata

Here's another great breakfast dish that can be prepped the night before and cooked in the morning, or even cooked the night before and served at room temperature. A frittata is basically a crustless quiche with endless variations; you can use any combination of vegetables, cheese and herbs that appeals to you. If you're watching your carbs, you can leave out the bread.

> "All happiness depends on a leisurely breakfast."
> —JOHN GUNTHER, JOURNALIST (1901–1970)

SERVES 4

6 large eggs

1 cup sour cream, *or* ½ pound cream cheese and ¼ cup light cream, *or* 1 cup
    ricotta cheese or goat cheese

2 cups cubed day-old bread *or* cooked potatoes

¼ cup chopped fresh basil or Italian flat-leaf parsley leaves

1 teaspoon kosher salt

1 teaspoon black pepper

1 tablespoon olive or canola oil

1 Spanish onion, chopped

2 garlic cloves, minced

2½ cups chopped broccoli or other green vegetable

Preheat the oven to 350 degrees.

Place the eggs, sour cream, ricotta, bread, basil, salt and pepper in a large bowl and gently mix.

Place a 9- or 10-inch ovenproof skillet over medium-high heat and when it is hot, add the oil. Add the onion and garlic and cook until golden, about 7 minutes. Add the broccoli and cook for 3 minutes.

Spoon the egg mixture over the vegetables and transfer the skillet to the oven.

Bake until the eggs are cooked and the top is golden, about 30 minutes. Serve hot or at room temperature.

TO MAKE THE NIGHT BEFORE: After you cook the vegetables, set them aside to cool. Add the cooled vegetables to the egg mixture in the bowl. Cover and refrigerate overnight. In the morning, preheat the oven to 350 degrees. Lightly butter an 8-inch springform or pie pan. Pour in the mixture and bake as above.

Metric Equivalencies

Liquid and dry measure equivalencies

CUSTOMARY	METRIC
¼ teaspoon	1.25 milliliters
½ teaspoon	2.5 milliliters
1 teaspoon	5 milliliters
1 tablespoon	15 milliliters
1 fluid ounce	30 milliliters
¼ cup	60 milliliters
⅓ cup	80 milliliters
½ cup	120 milliliters
1 cup	240 milliliters
1 pint *(2 cups)*	480 milliliters
1 quart *(4 cups, 32 ounces)*	960 milliliters *(.96 liter)*
1 gallon *(4 quarts)*	3.84 liters
1 ounce *(by weight)*	28 grams
¼ pound *(4 ounces)*	114 grams
1 pound *(16 ounces)*	454 grams
2.2 pounds	1 kilogram *(1,000 grams)*

Oven-Temperature Equivalencies

DESCRIPTION	FAHRENHEIT	CELSIUS
Cool	200	90
Very slow	250	120
Slow	300–325	150–160
Moderately slow	325–350	160–180
Moderate	350–375	180–190
Moderately hot	375–400	190–200
Hot	400–450	200–230
Very hot	450–500	230–260

Index